DATING FOR GROWN-UPS

To my wonderful girlfriends,

some of whom are lucky enough to be with their soulmates,

some of whom are still looking, and all of whom keep laughing,

whatever life throws at them.

Love you all,

Caroline

x

DATING FOR
GROWN-UPS

HOW TO FIND A NEW PARTNER WHEN YOU'RE OVER 40

CAROLINE DOUGHTY

WHITE
LADDER
PRESS
new tricks for old dogs

Dating for Grown-ups

This first edition published in Great Britain in 2008 by White Ladder Press,
a division of Crimson Publishing Ltd
Westminster House, Kew Road, Richmond, Surrey, TW9 2ND

16 15 14 13 12 11 10 09   10 9 8 7 6 5 4 3 2 1

A catalogue record for this book is available from the British library.

ISBN 978 1 905410 34 7

Designed and typeset by Julie Martin Ltd
Cover design by Julie Martin Ltd
Printed and bound in Turkey by Mega Printing

CONTENTS

ACKNOWLEDGEMENTS

With thanks to all the people who so bravely shared their dating experiences and stories with me for this book. Most names have been changed so I won't reveal them now – you know who you are and thank you. Thanks also to the professionals who gave their time to contribute to this book.

Thanks to Ellie and Laura who would gladly have their mother marry the plumber, fishman or any number of friends' dads if they weren't already taken ... I love your enthusiasm, if not all your choices, and I hope one day I'll find someone we can all agree on.

And thanks to Roni, Lez and everyone else at White Ladder for your encouragement, enthusiasm and for being such a great team to work with.

Introduction

You're single. You've already hit the big 40. And you want to share your life with someone else ... which means dating – something you may not have done for a very long time and something you never really expected to be doing at this time of life.

Though your heart can still flutter like a teenager's, your body is probably not in quite the same shape and your confidence may have taken a good few knocks over the years.

Perhaps you're sagging a bit in the middle, your roots may be inclined to silver or perhaps your hairline has got into a receding groove. And on top of all that, there's possibly a bit of 'emotional baggage' that you've gathered on your journey so far.

So how on earth are you going to meet a new partner? And who'd want to fall in love with you – with your saggy tummy, ex-partner and possibly some children thrown in for good measure?

Stop right there. This all sounds pretty negative doesn't it? Flab, grey hair, emotional baggage? Well, the truth is most of us, by the time we hit 40, have had at least one significant relationship and if that relationship has ended it's highly likely that you suffered in the process, whatever happened.

But you've come through that experience and are now ready to look for love again and for that you deserve congratulations – it's a brave step. And it's the most important one you can make if you are to find a new partner a bit later in life.

Let's kick off with a mental trick – from now on try thinking of your 'baggage' as 'knowledge' and it'll seem completely different. Everything that's happened to you has just helped you become more mature, more worldly-wise, and more sure of what it is you want and need to make you happy. No more baggage. Easy isn't it?

We all know the story. You're bowling along with your partner, thinking everything's just fine – it's possibly not quite as exciting as it once was, you seem to watch more telly and there's no sex on the kitchen table any more – but you think you're happy. Then bam, out of the blue, your partner tells you they've had enough and they're leaving you for someone else.

Or perhaps you met when you were very young and by the time you hit your mid-thirties you realised that you didn't like this grown-up person very much after all. She wasn't quite as funny as she was at 18 in the student union bar, he'd put on so much weight you didn't fancy him any more, or possibly he spent so much time at work he ended up being rather too attracted to the office trainee and forgot he had a wife who had been temporarily distracted by small children.

Or maybe you were dealt a really tough blow and now find yourself alone because the person you loved has died, leaving you widowed before you'd experienced much of what married life had to offer. It can take years to begin to feel single again, but you can get to the stage where you do want to share your life with someone special once more.

Whatever the reason, you're back in the dating game.

Nervous, excited, scared, hopeful, terrified, optimistic, full of dread ... we've probably all felt all of these emotions at some point and you're bound to feel them all again. At 70, the tingle of locking eyes with someone or sharing a first kiss is just as exciting as at 17, if not more so, because you are more aware of the undiscovered joys to come. So whenever you feel like giving up or get weary of trying to find your next true love, just remind yourself of that feeling as an inspiration to keep going.

Imagine you're about to go out on a date with someone you really like the look of. Maybe you were introduced by friends, perhaps you got chatting in a pub or at a sports event, maybe you met each other through an online dating site. However the introduction was made you're now about to go out and meet them in the flesh. You're probably quite excited – you're undoubtedly nervous. But the thing to remember is that they're feeling *exactly the same way*. Even if you're 40 or 50 or 60, whether you've raised a family, built a business or travelled the world, we all still feel pretty much the same when it comes to falling in love – which is, of course, what you hope will happen.

So how can this book help you?

It is going to remove the mystique that surrounds dating. There's no magic art to it, but there's no recipe for success either. By looking at all the ways that are available for you to meet someone new, not including wild student parties and clubbing because – thankfully – we've all outgrown them by now, it's going to give you some ideas about how you might go about finding love.

You may be wondering what qualifies me to tell you how to do this? Well, nothing really. Except that I've spoken to dozens of people who are actively dating, some who are jaded with the whole thing, some who've found love and happiness and professionals whose job it is to try and make matches. Oh, and I've done a bit of dating too.

When I was 26 I fell in love with my soulmate – a wonderful man I met at work. Everyone told us it was bad news to have a relationship with a colleague but we ignored them and went on to get married nearly four years later. I was thrilled – I'd had more than enough of living the Bridget Jones life despite having had a lot of fun. Nick and I had two lovely daughters and life was rosy, when he became ill with cancer. The dream bubble burst and Nick died a year later. I found myself suddenly, terribly, single again at the age of 34 – though to be honest it took years before I felt truly 'single'. I still felt married, but to a husband who just wasn't there any more.

And so, tentatively, I put a foot back into the murky water of dating in my late thirties, with two now rather boisterous and demanding children. And I discovered that it's a whole different ball game trying to date as a mature woman and a single parent to boot. Finding the energy to get dressed up, organise babysitting and get out is enough of a challenge before you even get into the hows and wheres of meeting a potential partner.

This book is not about me, although I have tried many of the ideas discussed later, without enormous success but with some rather amusing stories to tell along the way. I have, however, met people who have done rather well and met gorgeous, loving partners through websites, speed-dating and at singles parties. It does happen – it can be hard work, it can take a while or you can be lucky and be hit by cupid's arrow on day one. Anything's possible.

The only common thread, or rule, that I've discovered along the way is that you have to believe in yourself. If you are confident and believe this will work then it probably will. If you are filled with self-doubt then other people will only see negatives.

Dating is not about what you look like, what you do for a job, or how much money you have. It's about believing that there are people out there who will fall in love with you for who you are, and going out there and finding them.

And it shouldn't be as hard as some people make it sound. Let's look at some statistics.

There were approximately 155,000 divorces in the UK in 2005, which means 310,000 people became single again in that year alone.

The average age of divorce is now 43 for men and 41 for women, so if you're in your forties there are literally thousands of people coming back onto the singles scene every year. OK, so a lot of them won't immediately be looking for a new partner – some never will. And many of them will be bruised by the experience of a failed marriage.

There are few people who reach 40 who haven't had some sort of life experiences that have knocked them around a bit, whether they've been married or not. Things are certainly not as simple as they once were.

Yet because of working patterns and social pressures many people are thinking about settling down with a partner much later then they would have done 30 or 40 years ago, and women are thinking about having children later. Many have been busy with careers, travelling, studying and so on and haven't noticed the tick of the biological clock until they are nearing 40 – for men they're often in their forties before they realise they really want to settle down.

There are myriad reasons why many 'normal' people are still looking for their first life partner at 40 and these are not desperate, sad people who have never had a partner. They're just people who never found the 'right one' and are now seriously looking for someone to share their life with.

When you look around it may well appear that the world is full of couples. But there are an awful lot of single people, just like you, who are out there and also looking for a soulmate.

So this book is going to help you find out where they are, how you're going to meet them, and what to say when you finally walk through the door of that café for your first – and possibly life-changing – cup of coffee.

CHAPTER 1

ARE YOU READY?

Trying to find a new partner is all very well but are you actually ready to do it? And do you really *know* what you are looking for?

There's absolutely no point putting a killer photo of yourself on a website with a witty and clever profile and then getting cold feet every time someone emails you, or going along to a first date and spending the entire evening moaning about how badly your ex treated you.

If you are going to embark on the dating game, the first things to do are decide if you are really ready to do this – if you're not it just won't work – and think seriously about what it is you are looking for.

Many people over 40 who start taking dating seriously

are looking for a 'life partner', someone they can settle down with, perhaps start a family with or help each other with the children they already have, someone they can grow old with.

Others are just looking to have some fun. They may have been through a really difficult time and just want to let their hair down a bit and learn how to laugh again. They may have come out of an unhappy marriage and don't want to get involved in a serious relationship again. They may want some occasional company for going out or they may just want to have sex.

All these scenarios are realistic and you need to be aware of them before you start dating. All of them are perfectly acceptable and if you're clear about what it is you're looking for, you're more likely to find it.

I've lost count of the number of people who've told me they've started internet dating – just one of the methods we're going to talk about – and have found that people either don't respond to emails, or they will exchange a few and then suddenly the other person 'disappears' without giving a reason.

Or there are the people who exchange a few emails, proceed to a phone call and then hang up mid-call. It happened to me and he was never heard from again. Or they never ring back despite sounding fairly interested on the first call.

You're then left wondering what you said to put them off, what you did wrong, and having a confidence crisis at the moment you need it least.

It could well be that they have got cold feet about dating anyone, they're already in a relationship with someone else, or they are simply chatting to several different people and decide to pursue things with someone else. However, most decent people say they'd much rather be told what's going on than be suddenly 'dropped' by someone who really isn't taking it seriously at all.

"I got this advice early on when I started dating – and the guy that told me knew I wasn't ready to date and that I really wasn't open to the idea at all. He told me to take it seriously, in the nicest possible way, and I have to say I think I needed to be told that. I didn't date for another year after that, but by then I really was ready," says Denise, *who ended up being pretty successful at going on dates but in the end fell in love with a friend.*

"Remember that any person who responds to you has feelings too – they will feel rejection if you stand them up,

don't respond to emails etc. They will also have put thought and energy into responding to you, and will also get nervous before meeting you. Remember to treat everyone as you would want to be treated."

In terms of knowing what you're looking for, I don't mean knowing that the man you're looking for has to be 5ft 11in tall, or the woman you're searching for has to have green eyes. What I mean is: are you looking for a relationship? Do you want to widen your social circle and make new friends? Or are you simply trying to find someone to have some adult fun with?

The expert's view

"We get a lot of people who are very fussy, hard to please and have long shopping lists of what they want. We say tear it up – you can't do it that way. Don't draw up the specifics of a man you want to meet. If you limit yourself at the beginning that's crazy." *Mary Balfour, of introduction agency Drawing Down the Moon*

There seem to be a large number of people playing the dating game who really don't know what it is they want. Many people join internet sites to expand their social circle and make new friends, with dating really not being uppermost in their mind at all.

Several sites have forums where you can go and chat to other people about literally anything: from what laptop to buy to the day's news events. It's amazing what people will find to talk about and you could, literally, spend days reading these conversations let alone taking part in them.

But if dating is what you're after, then try and concentrate on that and don't let yourself get too distracted.

I've spoken to many people who decided it was time to take dating seriously, signed up to some internet sites, went speed dating or attended some singles events and then, hey presto! They met their partner in the supermarket, or at a friend's house, or in the pub.

Often if you change your mindset and say to yourself that you are going to sort out this one area of your life that we so often ignore, then you'll meet a new partner just 'by chance'. Except it's not really chance. Consider this: when you decide to look for a new job you begin to notice opportunities, pick up bits of conversation about where there might be vacancies and enquire amongst the people you know about whether they know of anything suitable.

Likewise if you're going to move house you become

aware of what's on the market, you notice estate agents' signs where before you've walked straight past them, you suddenly see stories in the newspaper about the property market that never interested you before.

Well, so it is with dating. Get into the right mindset, start taking it seriously and you'll be amazed at how many opportunities you can come up with to meet people and how people will respond to you. If you're open to the possibility that anyone you meet might be the right one for you, then the world suddenly looks very different.

"You have to be quite realistic about what your expectations are – you get back what you put in. If you put some effort in, you get more out of it." Annette, 56

The expert's view

Srimati is a life coach and runs a course entitled 'Are you ready for love?', which came about when she realised that many people who go for life or career coaching have an unfulfilling love life and would like help to get it back on track. There seemed to be a need to cater specifically for this and her weekend course has been well received.

"People don't want to recreate the mistakes they have

made before," she says. "The course is about developing the right attitudes. The best preparation is to do the inner work first. The mechanics (of how you meet someone) are secondary.

"I get people to reassess where they're at in relation to having a partner. Then I encourage them to do a bit of visualisation of what would be their ideal. It gives them permission to want what they want. Many people feel they don't deserve it or it's not possible, or that the man or woman they want to meet doesn't exist. We also look at all the beliefs, attitudes and fears that come up, such as men won't commit or women are all too cold."

Srimati actively encourages people to think of 50 reasons why they would make a brilliant partner and what they have to offer. She also suggests doing a bit of planning and goal-setting – whether it be going out more, doing some assertiveness training, finding a friend to go out with or losing some weight. It's all about being positive and clear about your intentions, she says, and laying fears aside.

"There's a difference between men and women. Men hang on to the past much more. They're more hurt by what's happened to them, more attached to their exes. Women seem to be able to do their grieving and forgiv-

ing and move on, but men are often not really ready –
they don't talk about stuff so they have no way of pro-
cessing their baggage."

Sarah did some coaching when she decided that she really wanted to 'unstick' her love life and start meeting
more men. Her coach encouraged her to think about
where she wanted to be in terms of a relationship in one
year, in three years and in five years. Then she made her
say it out loud.

*"Being able to say 'I want to be in a loving, stable rela-
tionship' out loud was really hard at first – but it did
make me admit to myself what it was I really wanted
and being forced to say it out loud made it more real."*
Sarah

So be bold – think hard about what it is you are looking
for, and don't be afraid to take some positive steps to
begin that journey. Be brutally honest about what it is
you have to offer someone and be clear about what you
want back. You're more likely to be successful if you
know what you're looking for.

CHAPTER 2

INTERNET DATING

Probably the most well-known form of dating these days is internet dating – but if you've come out of a 20-year marriage it's something you won't have had experience of when you were dating in the 1970s or '80s.

There are dozens of mainstream dating websites in the UK, and more that cater for very specific tastes. It's impossible to get an exact figure but millions of people have registered with dating sites and thousands are actively using them every day. A quick glance is enough to prove that many of them are pretty normal, sociable, good-looking adults rather than a bunch of no-hopers making a last ditch attempt at finding a partner.

Internet dating has gone mainstream. For young people

it's almost cool and the stigma that surrounded it 10 years ago when it was new has all but gone. Everywhere you look – in newspapers, magazines, on buses, trains and billboards – you see adverts for websites that promise to change your life.

The expert's view

"In the last few years older people are coming onto dating sites more and more. As broadband becomes more widespread and as computers become cheaper there are a lot more older people on the internet. One of the largest increasing segments is the 50-plus age bracket."
Andy Maccabe, at LoveandFriends.com

Most sites cater for the general public, but there are now dating sites for sporty people, Jewish people, Muslims and born-again Christians. There's Conservative dating, green dating, senior dating, millionaire dating, single parent dating, dog lovers' dating ... and more if you have adventurous sexual tendencies.

But for now, we're going to concentrate on mainstream dating sites that most people will be more likely to aim for. The two biggies in the UK are Dating Direct and Match.com. Both claim thousands of members and have a really good geographic spread, thanks to blanket

advertising and big budgets. They're also both international, so if you fancied finding a friend in Papua New
Guinea you might well be able to do it through them.

Then there are the newspaper sites – Guardian
Soulmates, Telegraph dating, Times Online encounters
– and loveandfriends.com. These claim to capture a
more educated, well-read class of dater than the mass-
market sites, and obviously the newspaper sites are
going to capture like-minded customers. You're far more
likely to meet a Conservative voter if you choose
Telegraph dating and if green credentials are important
to you then stick with Guardian Soulmates.

The Sun also has a dating site and while no one would
claim that the most intelligent daters will be found on
there, at least you're quite likely to know what you'll get
if you log on. Call it natural selection.

The newspaper sites also claim a lot of users – they obviously have the power of advertising through their papers
and can leverage this against some of the smaller, inde-
pendent dating sites.

Though most claim to be national, many are heavily
concentrated in the south-east of the UK and you will
find that as soon as you're more than 50 miles outside

of London there is a much smaller pool of fishes swimming around in the online sea.

The expert's view

"People were doing internet dating in London while in the rest of the country people thought it was just for saddos. London follows America and cities also tend to attract more single people. The bigger, the more advanced the city, the more people have computers, and they tend also to be early adopters of technology." *Andy Maccabe, LoveandFriends.com.*

Depending on who you ask, internet dating can be a real boost to the ego, great fun or an incredible waste of time. A quarter of the people who responded to our survey said they found it too time-consuming (24%) and 16% said they hated it.

But love it or loathe it, it's a great way to meet people you wouldn't normally come across in your day to day life and, taken in the right spirit, it can be a lot of fun.

Your feelings towards internet dating are likely to go through phases – you will have a great time for a while, then get fed up with it. You will hate it at times and take a break from it completely, then go back to it with renewed enthusiasm. It's quite normal and it's far better to just 'hide' your photo and profile for a while when you've had enough, stop thinking about it for a few weeks, go and do other things and then come back to it when you're ready for another round of dating.

So what exactly is it all about?

What it involves

First you have to write your profile, then you have to find a decent photo of yourself or ask a friend to take one. Believe me, there's nothing more ridiculous than dressing yourself up and then posing for a friend to take photos that you know are going to be used to advertise yourself to strangers.

I had a photo session like this once for a friend. We chose a top, took pictures with lipstick and without, hair up, hair down. We did end up with a couple of good shots and her hit rate went up dramatically on a website afterwards – probably because her hair was blonder than in the previous photos. But you do have to know someone pretty well before you can ask them to go along with all this.

Once you've taken a photo you have to upload it to the

site – and you can guarantee that this process will take at least one whole evening. First there's that tricky bit of remembering how to connect the camera to the computer (if you can find the cable), then downloading the right picture, trying not to get distracted by looking at lots of other pictures on your computer, then editing it a bit to crop it, make it brighter and so on, then waiting for it to upload to the site. Then you may find out it's the wrong format and have to go back to your editing software to save it in a different format. Saving it with the .jpg extension is usually best as most dating sites accept photos in this format.

Now you have to be prepared for match.com to decide it doesn't like the picture you've chosen to be your main profile photo and it will pick another. I don't know whether it's a real human being that does this but I doubt it. I imagine their computers judge photos in a similar way to the new passport rules – it has to be a clear shot, facing the camera and it doesn't like it if you're looking sideways or are too far away. So don't be too clever and avoid hats and sunglasses.

Finally your photo is up on your profile and now you can start searching for a man or woman who catches your eye. This is where the real time-wasting begins.

You enter your search criteria and let the computer do its magic. But how demanding should you be? You know you like your dates to be over 5ft 10ins, but could you be ruling out the man of your dreams who just happens to be 5ft 9?ins? Ideally you want someone who's been to university like you, but maybe your dream woman left school at 18 and then did professional training instead, so you'd be ruling her out too.

There's no right or wrong answer to this one, but my advice is don't be too specific. I did a search once and rang a friend saying "Help! I can only find eight men in the whole of Devon!" Later that evening she emailed me a list of 10 whose profiles I hadn't even seen and a couple of them led to interesting conversations (though sadly nothing more exciting to report).

SEARCHING FOR YOUR SOULMATE

Start with a broad search, though if you type 'any' for every single category you will end up trawling through hundreds of profiles. So pick the things that are most important to you and go easy on the others.

You may not get very good results, so it's worth fiddling about with your search criteria a bit. Change the age group and see who pops up – you could be surprised.

You should also keep in mind that people do lie about their age on internet dating sites so someone may well be a little older than they say they are. And don't rule out too many people by age.

"I'm 59 and he was 48 when I met him – he had never looked at my profile and I may never have looked at him." Jean, who met her current partner Steve through chatting on a dating website forum. They then met at a social event and began exchanging emails.

"He's 10 years older than me – I'd normally have looked at men six to seven years older, but not quite 10. Perhaps that's where I've been going wrong all these years!" Annette, who has been with Jim for six months since meeting him online

I have heard that half the people on internet sites lie about their age and a third of the men are married. Obviously there's no way of knowing how true either of these assumptions are, but it's safe to say you should be aware of the tricks people play and just be open to the possibility that people may doctor their date of birth to try and appeal to more people.

The expert's view

"Men always want someone a bit younger and women over 40 tend to be quite keen on men the same age or younger. Few want a man more than five years older, but you can be flexible about age." *Mary Balfour*

There are other reasons people will rule you out – some of them quite bizarre.

"Sadly I have sifted people out because of the wallpaper behind them in their photo. Though I reckon if they had looked more attractive to me, their wallpaper may not have mattered quite so much." Denise

Having put your profile up and done some searches, one of the things that's quite likely to happen is that you will get emails from people who you don't really like the look of. What do you do? It's hard to say to someone who's plucked up the courage to email you that you're not interested, but the one thing you have to be if you're going to do internet dating is thick-skinned.

To be honest this is not a natural process for anyone – emailing strangers and judging people on a grainy photo or a few tick boxes about their 'character' before ever meeting them. You have to be prepared to step outside your comfort zone to do this – but fear not, once you've got into the swing of it it does become easier.

> *"I was shocked to discover that I have been registered on JDate.com since 2000 I think, and in all that time there was just one guy that I wanted to have more than two dates with. Each time I am ready to terminate my membership one of my friends goes and gets bloody engaged to someone they met online. This always breaks my resolve,"*
> Jan, who is still persevering

Time to start emailing

Those first few emails are hard, and the first knock-back from someone you quite like the look of is also tough. But you get used to it and you find ways of saying no to people. It's also worth remembering that there's no point getting hung up on the people who don't want to pursue your email exchange – there are plenty of others out there and the chances are they weren't right for you anyway.

If you are approached by someone you don't like the look of, how do you handle it? You can take the direct approach of "I'm sorry I was looking for someone younger" but that's probably not the kindest knock-back to give someone. I did that when I was new to the game, thinking honesty was the best policy, but the man in question was none too pleased and I did think afterwards it was a little unfair. After all, if I had really liked the look of him I wouldn't have cared nearly as much about his age.

It's probably best to say that you're already talking to someone else on the site and you don't want to complicate things at the moment, which is a rejection, but not an outright rejection on the basis of a their photo. Let people down gently and, if you can, do reply to people's emails rather than just ignore the ones you don't like the look of. Somehow it seems unfair when that person has plucked up the courage to email you just simply to put it in the trash and ignore them.

"There were occasions when I would have a pop at someone. I'd say 'I would have appreciated something back, even if it was a polite sod off'. And I've been completely mystified on occasions too. I've felt like saying 'you have clearly ignored everything I've said on my profile'."
Philip, 47

So yes, there are going to be odd emails. And emails from people you really don't want to talk to but, let's face it, this is far less intimidating than having someone offer to buy you a drink in a bar when they've obviously put away one too many beers and you don't like the look of them.

"You meet the same cross section of people you meet in any other sector. There are the weirdos, the saddos, the nutters and the predators but there are also ordinary people. Women think it's risky, but in what way is it risky? If you meet people in a pub you know nothing about them, you have had a few drinks yourself and are potentially vulnerable and it's far more risky. Online you find out far more about them before you meet them, and you can arrange to talk to someone over the phone. Nobody can stalk you by telephone, you can find out a lot about somebody easily by talking to them and there's no risk. I think in many ways it's safer than any other means of meeting people." Philip

"I have had some extraordinary responses on the internet. There was a guy who worked on an oil rig in Brazil who sent some rather tasteless photos. And a friend of mine got some photographs from a guy and there was one of him posing in his underpants. What would make him think that any woman would find that attractive?" Annette

So assuming that you are quite normal and not about to indulge someone with photos of you posing in your smalls, should you approach people or wait for them to come to you?

If you're going to do internet dating, then you might as well go for it – Prince Charming is unlikely to appear from out of the blue. So the best advice is to pick out a few people you like the look of and just say hello. You really don't need to be too clever in your first email. Once they get an email from you they'll be intrigued – they'll look at your profile, look again more carefully if they've already seen it and if they're a decent human being they'll think about your approach. The fact you've said hello means you're interested enough to strike up a conversation and, just like with real life conversation with strangers, it generally gets easier once the ice is broken.

Imagine you're at a friend's party and you're standing by the food table or getting a drink and someone you quite like the look of wanders up or is standing next to you. What do you do? You have a choice – you can either smile sheepishly and hope he or she will talk to you. If they don't you end up sloping off thinking 'damn, I missed my chance'. Or you can be really brave and say "Hi! This food looks delicious doesn't it?" It's not rocket science, but it breaks the ice and if they are at all interested in talking to you they'll pick up your lead and start talking. And you're off.

So just treat internet dating the same way. Break that ice and you're on your way.

The expert's view

"Neither sex is very good at making that first move. Eighty percent of people say they want the other person to make the first move – that creates a stalemate. I think people don't know what to say." *Fiona Maclean who runs a couple of internet dating sites*

Of course one possibility is that you'll steel yourself, be really brave, craft a witty but casual-sounding email and fire it off only to find that a week later your dream date has read the mail but not replied to it.

What does this mean?

The expert's view

"People hesitate to reply because they don't want to tell the truth – you're too old, you're too young, or you've got kids." *Fiona Maclean*

Maybe they weren't particularly interested and were just

too rude to bother replying (in which case you wouldn't want to date them anyway); or they're talking to other people on the site and are thinking 'maybe I'll reply if it doesn't go anywhere with him/her'; or thirdly they are trying to think of something witty to respond with. And if that takes them several days they're probably not going to be much fun to go out with anyway.

Others will just find it easier to say nothing than to make up an excuse.

Some sites will automatically delete emails a few days after you've read them, so be wary of reading an email quickly when you're in a hurry and thinking 'I'll write back later when I've got more time' because you may not be able to find the email again later.

If someone contacts you, do the decent thing and reply. It doesn't really matter what you say, but say something.

"My latest attempt was through Guardian Soulmates. I had no response from anybody I messaged, let alone had any guys get in touch with me having seen my photo (which I thought was rather good). In the end I resigned – and changed my details. They then began with the headline 'Guys, you can all sod off.' And instead of my

profile I had a little bit of a rant about 'do as you would be done by' being a good maxim for life and how it was extremely rude not to reply to somebody who'd emailed you, and why did they think that kind of behaviour was acceptable because it wasn't.

"To get no response from anyone makes you doubt yourself terribly – then you read all this stuff about how you won't find anybody until you learn to love yourself first, which is pretty much impossible when you are feeling vulnerable." Melanie, 53

"I found the hardest thing about the site was being able to strike that balance between looking interested and not appearing desperate. You email him, he emails back. Just simple 'hello'-type emails. So you reply, say a bit more, try and be witty but not look like some eager puppy desperate for attention. This might go on for a couple of days and then suddenly – silence! He hasn't replied to your latest email but you can tell through the site that he's read it. So what do you do? How long do you wait before you badger him again and ask why he didn't reply? Do you just sulk and never contact him again? Or do you take the direct approach and ask him why he's gone quiet? Always a risk, because he might tell you something you really didn't want to hear." Another Soulmates user

There is no easy answer to this one, honesty perhaps not always being the kindest policy. There are times when you just have to be guided by your common sense and your own gut feeling on how the conversation was going.

One feature of some sites that is really useful is the 'stock answers' that you can choose to send to someone you don't want to get into conversation with. They say things like "Thanks but I'm already talking to someone" or "Thanks but I think I've found my match". It's a bit of a cop-out, but still better than silence.

Not all experiences online are pleasant and you do have to be prepared to meet some toads before you'll find your prince or princess.

"I met a man who said he was separated from his wife, only to discover that he meant that he was sleeping in the spare bedroom and hoping to reconcile; then a man who weighed nearly 300 pounds who openly criticized me for being a size 16; and thirdly a guy who disappeared into the ether after the fifth date when I told him that I really thought it was time for him to tell me his last name. I gave up after that." Stephanie

GETTING THE PROFILE RIGHT

So just how do you write a decent profile that will make you sound attractive, funny and the kind of person your soulmate really wants to meet?

Selling yourself is probably the hardest thing to do and there are no rules, but let's look at some guidelines.

First, you want to get across a bit of your personality. Nearly everyone says they like good food, wine and conversation. Well most people do, don't they? Saying that really isn't going to give anything interesting away about you – who you are, what makes you tick, what makes you happy?

Before you even start to write your profile think hard about who you are and what you want out of a partner and/or relationship.

How do you like spending your time? Are you an indoors or outdoors sort of person? Are you sporty, arty or musical? A bookworm, film buff or culture vulture? Do you love spending your holidays looking around ruined architecture or do you like sitting by a pool reading the latest Ian Rankin? Are you a vegan? A classical cellist? Is your garage the place where you store your aging drum kit or your prized Aston Martin? These are the things that will give more of a flavour of the kind of person you really are.

Let's face it – nearly all of us, past the age of 40, have done the pubbing and clubbing thing. We all like a good night out, some more often than others, but most of us would be happy to spend the odd evening inside, with someone we love, curled up on the sofa watching a good movie and sharing a bottle of nice wine. I've given up on the number of profiles I've seen which say 'evenings in with DVD and bottle of red'. It says nothing about you, except possibly that you don't hit the town every single night of the week.

One brilliant profile I read had a list of 'things I like' and 'things I hate' which is becoming more common. One of the things he hated? "Having a good hair day when you're not going anywhere." OK, so it's not worthy of a Pulitzer Prize, but it's an original line that makes you think 'Oh yes! I hate that too.'

One woman wrote: "I must confess that I have tried on a tea cosy when left alone in a room with it when I was younger and still have that wee daft streak in me."

Another said: "I put something about football into my profile. It was the time of the World Cup and I got about

100 replies. A woman who likes football was clearly an attractive proposition!"

Another one that caught my eye said: "I like vintage clothes shopping and I own seven pairs of cowboy boots. It's getting beyond a joke. My books and CDs are taking over my life, well my shelf space at least." It shows great personality and is a far more interesting way of saying she likes reading and listening to music.

Match.com has a rather nifty 'tagging' feature which allows you to choose single words that you believe sum you up. Some of the most popular are 'music, movies, swimming, walking, brownhair, blueeyes'. But the more original that say much more about a person include 'crispcleanair', 'homemadepastries', 'harleyenthusiast', and 'glastonburyfan'. You can choose as many as you like, and search on these terms too, so it helps narrow down a search and could help find someone who shares a particularly novel pastime if you have one. Tallgirl, surfer, sarcasticwit and starwarsfreak are others.

Match.com says: "Since tags are short, they allow online daters to pack a lot of their interests and personality into their profile without making viewers' eyes glaze over." What's more, since you can search by tags, they help people with eclectic interests connect.

The expert's view

"There may be a lot of options you'd like to search by, but traditional online dating searches don't always give you that option. I've often lamented that I can't search for a geek who likes both punk and jazz," says Alyssa Wodtke, author of *Truth, Lies, and Online Dating: Secrets to Finding Romance on the Internet.* "The tagging feature lets the music geek I'm looking for tag himself as such — and lets me find him. Tags are the perfect way to find that make-or-break quality you may be looking for in a mate."

Some tags you come up with can, and should, be purely for fun. "The trick in online dating is to make yourself stand out, and unusual tags can help you in this goal," says Wodtke. So, ask yourself what thoughts or habits make you truly unusual, whether that's LovePoppingBubblewrap or AfraidofClowns. "It's never a bad idea to show who you really are because you're more likely to find someone who will like you for who you really are," explains Wodtke. "And that's everyone's ultimate goal."

FINALLY YOU STRIKE GOLD

If you've had days, or possibly weeks, of opening messages warily in case yet another one says "Sorry, I've met someone else on here" or, worse, "I don't think you're what I'm looking for," the excitement of getting a reply from someone you've contacted that says "Fancy a chat? Here's my number" can be enough to make you catch your breath in front of the screen.

If you do get that message from someone you like the look of, then pick up the phone. Remember this is still less scary than talking to a stranger in a bar. It's probably a good idea, though, to hide your phone number by dialling 141 before their telephone number, just in case.

You can cover more ground in one half-hour phone call than in a hundred emails and you'll also hear their voice, which can instantly convey far more than all those emails ever could.

If he or she makes you laugh, you're on to a good thing. At least you know that if you meet up you're likely to have an enjoyable evening, even if it doesn't lead to love.

And remember, when you're talking to someone, be interested in what they're saying, ask questions and don't view it as a golden opportunity to tell them everything about yourself that you find fascinating.

Men (sorry guys) do tend to be the experts at this. They'll ask a question, you'll begin to answer and they'll say "Oh yes, I know just what you mean. When I was working at xxx" or "When I went there on holiday I found ..." It's not a winner, guys. It just makes you sound self-obsessed and totally uninterested in what your potential date has to say. Which, take it from me, is not a good way to flatter a woman's ego.

Whole books have been written about the 'art' of internet dating and I've heard it described as art, science and skill. It's perhaps not that complicated, but here are a few guidelines that will hopefully help you succeed:

◆ Always use a good photo. A natural shot is best, not a posed 'studio' shot.

◆ Write an interesting profile (see next page).

◆ Be honest with all your answers – you'll be found out sooner or later and it's better to start any relationship with a basis of honesty and trust.

◆ Ask your friends to do some searches for you – you'll be surprised who they find.

◆ Be prepared to take time off if you're getting fed up and go back to it when you're more enthusiastic.

◆ Be prepared to start conversations with people, don't wait for them to contact you.

- ◆ Try and reply to the emails you get – unless you're receiving dozens every day.

- ◆ Try and move to the phone or meet for a coffee fairly quickly – spending days or weeks emailing each other isn't going to get you anywhere.

- ◆ Be willing to talk to several people at once – it's allowed and it's what most other people on dating sites are doing. Keep your options open.

- ◆ Set yourself a time limit, say an hour a day, to be on the site. Don't get obsessive about checking for emails – this is only one part of your life and it's important to get out and do other things as well.

- ◆ If someone refuses to give you a home telephone number, will only meet during the week and turns their mobile off a lot of the time, they could be in a relationship already so use your common sense.

Most of the dating websites will give you advice on how to write a good profile and each site is different in the way it presents information. But here are a few general guidelines that will apply to all the sites:

- ◆ Make sure you tick the right boxes when you're filling in the form. If you say you're 4ft 6ins tall, women may hesitate to contact you.

◆ Tick as many of them as you can – if your profile is full of blanks it looks as if you couldn't be bothered or you don't want to reveal anything about yourself, which won't make people feel confident about who you are.

◆ If you choose not to display a photograph because of the job you do (many teachers and doctors have told me they wouldn't want pupils or patients seeing them on such a site), then explain and say you'd be happy to send one on request. People will understand and respect this.

◆ Use questions in your profile. If you say 'My favourite thing to do on a wet Sunday afternoon is to escape into the nearest cinema – what's yours?' then you've immediately given people something to say in that initial email which is very tricky to write.

◆ Don't use a makeover shot as your photo. Many men I've spoken to said they were suspicious of them because the women they'd met who'd used them looked nothing like that in real life. It's far better to use a natural, realistic shot.

◆ When you describe your perfect match give a few indicators of what you're looking for and don't leave all the boxes blank. If you do, it just looks as if you'd date anyone and you're not at all fussy, which doesn't make you look very interesting.

Jean met Steve while chatting on the forums on Love and Friends in June 2007. They chatted online for a while, then started talking by phone.

"There's a virtual bar on the site where people pop in and chat to each other. He came in there one night and seemed to be a really nice guy.

He was coming to a party in Abingdon arranged by one of the women on the forum. I was there reasonably early on the Saturday. He'd already said online that he was going to meet his sister first, to introduce her to the new love of his life so I thought he'd met someone and I was really pleased for him.

When he arrived I gave him a hug and asked where she was. He looked surprised and realised what I meant. He said 'She's in the car park – she's my new motorbike!'

That was it really for the weekend – I didn't see him much more than that and didn't dance with him. I didn't think any more of it really.

Then he came on the site and was chatting about his

daughter's wedding and I asked him to talk to me on msn. We got friendly on msn and it was as if we'd known each other for ever. He can do small-talk really well for a bloke and he listens too.

Then it was my birthday and I said if you want you can ring me. He rang me and chatted to me for five hours, from 12.30am to 5.30 in the morning. He made me laugh and I made him laugh. He said do you mind if I ring you again?

As a man he's very good about keeping in touch. He sends a text to say he's home from work every day and rings me every evening.

I was planning a camping event and he asked if he could come down a day early from Edinburgh, where he lives. We both said let's have a good friendship and see where it goes from there.

One box he doesn't tick is that he's smaller than me. I'm 5ft 8^1/$_2$ins and he's 5ft 5ins. He calls me amazon! That's been the weirdest thing.

I'm 59 and he was 48 when I met him but it's just been so easy. He would never have looked at my profile and I may never have looked at him. But I feel such contentment and so at ease with him. I've suggested he comes down here and I'm happy to talk about doing something together in Lincolnshire.

It's a very easy relationship. My children think he's lovely. I've always said who's going to want me because I'm a bit zany – a bit unusual. It's good to find someone who accepts my unusualness."

Chapter 3

Speed dating

This one is a bit of a new craze. Most people back in the dating game after a break of a few years won't have tried this before and in some respects the idea is quite bizarre.

You go to a bar, or club or restaurant where there should be, if it's a well-organised event, the same number of men and women. They should also be within a certain age range that corresponds to what you're looking for.

The women take their places at tables, spread out around the room. The men then each sit down opposite one woman and a bell rings. You have three minutes to get to know your 'speed date' and the bell then rings again. You have a minute to scribble some notes and the men move round to sit down in front of the next date.

Off you go again, and so on for 20 or 25 people. Hopefully you'll get a break in the middle for a drink.

Some people say it's a great way to meet lots of potential dates in one evening, flirt with loads of different people, practise your chat-up lines and come away with the possibility of lots of 'real' dates to follow.

Others would say it's like doing 20 or 30 mini job interviews with a bunch of people you'd never dream of dating and the whole process is quite depressing.

> *"Speed dating was the most fun thing I've done and the most successful as you get to see if there is that original attraction. I thought I had met a nice guy on two separate occasions but they never worked out that way. But it is a really good way to realise that there are some decent single guys and it is nice to know that everyone you are chatting to is in the same situation. There's no wondering if their girlfriend has just nipped to the loo."* Claire

There are a few things to watch out for when you go speed dating. If you can go to an evening that has a theme you're probably more likely to meet people you'll at least have something in common with. Some organisations arrange evenings for graduate professionals, most split people up into age groups (though be prepared for people to sneak into different groups) and others run evenings for Asian Muslims, Christians, or Jewish daters (if you live in London).

There's no reason to say you'll have anything in common with any of the people you'll meet at a speed dating evening but it's a great way to practise talking to new people if you're not used to it, and it does have the potential to be a lot of fun.

"It's fun, but it's very random. There is only a score of potential dates and no reason why you should have anything much in common with them." Matt

Of course one of the problems with speed dating is that while you get to meet 20 or 30 people of the opposite sex, you're not without your own competition on the night.

"If you meet someone you like, you don't want to move on and you don't want her to meet someone when you do." Andy

One tip that might be worth using if you decide to go speed dating is to try and go with a friend of the opposite sex if possible. This way you get a break half-way round when you're opposite each other and can have a laugh discussing your progress. If you go with a friend of the same sex you might end up fancying the same person.

It can be quite a challenge to think of interesting things to say to 20 strangers, one after the other. But don't ask them all the same question because by the end of the evening you really will sound as though you're talking from a script.

The expert's view

The experts at speeddater.co.uk, the UK's biggest speed dating organisation, suggest that you should do three things when you introduce yourself on a speed date.

Compliment, ask a question and then introduce yourself. That doesn't sound entirely natural but it's all about putting the other person at ease and building their confidence.

People do like to be praised, so try and spot something they've spent a lot of money or effort on around their appearance and tell them you like it. Obviously the aim is not to sit there looking them up and down and trying to work out how much their shirt cost, but a simple "I really like your tie" comment might be enough to break the ice.

It's probably a good idea not to worry too much about your opening line though – it's unlikely that one line will win you a date, so just aim to open up an interesting conversation and if you can make them laugh, so much the better.

Smile, face them, look them in the eye and ask a fairly innocuous question such as: "How has your day been? What do you do for fun when you're not here?"

Some experts say that what you utter at the very beginning isn't that important because you're both busy checking each other out on so many different levels that the words rarely make a difference. And a lot of this happens at a subconscious level – it's to do with physical attraction, body language and chemistry.

Others say your date might decide in seconds if you're worth making the effort with, so you have to get it right from the off.

But thinking about it – how many times do you remember the first words one of your ex-boyfriends or girlfriends ever said to you? You may remember where you met, but what they said is unlikely to have stuck in your mind. It's really not worth getting completely hung up on your opening gambit.

Also bear in mind that if you are going to click as friends, it will happen fairly quickly. If it feels like hard work it's probably never going to work and this is only speed dating – it's not as though you're trying to impress the person who's going to sit at the desk beside you for the next five years.

So what do you talk about?

Asking your date about themselves is a good start – it'll make them feel you're interested enough to get to know them a bit. But remember they'll want to get to know you too, so the conversation has to go both ways.

Keep it light and encourage them to open up a bit, but don't interrogate them. Try and find out what excites them or what they find fun. If their face lights up when they mention something then ask about it – a hobby, pet or job.

Get good at giving compliments without sounding creepy – nothing too personal but enough to make them feel good about themselves.

"It took me two attempts at speed dating to get what it was all about and to get it kind of right. The first time I went I picked a category where I was in the older half. I hadn't thought about it but I was hopeful that I would

find a nice date. Realistically, though, I was a girl – and the boys wanted the younger girls (some things are clichéd for a reason). I put in loads of energy and I came out knackered and with no dates. I also didn't chat much in between. It was quite a serious approach. The second time I went I was in the younger half of the age group – and guess what? This cliché worked better for me! I went with two friends – a man and a woman. When I got to my male friend I had a giggle half-way round and came back refreshed. I'm sure other men saw me with a man and realised they had competition and that I had a good laugh. I didn't take it very seriously and I didn't put so much into it, so I wasn't so drained. I had a few dates from that evening and it was fun to meet up afterwards because talking about dating gives you something in common to start with." Suzie

Stephanie went speed dating in a bar in central London. She said the women were all ages, some well over 40 and the men were early to mid-30s with a few "who were fooling themselves". It was not, it turned out, a very good experience.

"You walk around with your overpriced drink and the guys are picking out the few women they consider to be beautiful. Most of the women were average looking, most

of the men were average looking – but the difference was the men didn't know they were average. It was absolutely unnatural – it was weird.

"People say it's a fun alternative than going into a bar. Bullshit – it's more like a meat market. It felt so unnatural, so forced. Some of the guys you could see coming up to your table thinking 'Oh no, not her' – and that's just horrendous.

"No one could maintain eye contact for long because they were too busy scoping out the room and seeing if someone 'better' was around. The organisers seemed clueless and the participants seemed desperate. Based on my experience, I don't see speed dating as the solution for our declining birth rate." Stephanie

The concept is possibly one that suits men more than women – the chance to chat up dozens of women on the same night. But however you feel about it as a gimmick, it can be a good evening out – more fun if you go with a friend or two – and is certainly great for practising how to talk to strangers, especially if you're out of the habit. Beyond that, you'd have to be pretty lucky to meet the love of your life. But it does happen.

Just over a third (36%) of the people who filled in our

survey had tried speed dating. Their reactions were fairly mixed, from those who absolutely hated it to those who had a fun time. Comments included: interesting, fun, unremarkable, superficial and tiring.

"I can see it working for people quite well, as those who go speed dating are sufficiently ready for a relationship that they can actually meet people face-to-face. This is compared to internet dating which I suspect suits people who are still hiding to an extent." Rosa

"I got a snog at every event I've been to, which is three now." Laura, who didn't meet any potential partners, but did have a good time

The general consensus is that you need to be fairly confident to go into a room full of strangers, turn on the charm, make people laugh and come out not feeling like you've been for the world's most gruelling interview.

But what on earth do you say when you only have three minutes to get across your best side *and* find out about the other person? Psychologist Professor Richard Wiseman from the University of Hertfordshire conducted an experiment to find out what the most successful chat-up lines were among people who did speed-dating.

The most successful daters used lines such as "What is

your favourite pizza topping?" and "Who would you be if you were going on Stars in Your Eyes?"

Both these lines are fairly light-hearted open questions, giving the other person the chance to make a joke, reveal something about themselves or just have a laugh.

The worst lines were "I have a PhD in computing" and "My best friend is a helicopter pilot." Hard, really, to think of a response to either.

Wiseman ran the experiment with 100 people aged 22 to 45 at the Edinburgh International Science Festival and said it showed that almost half the women made decisions about potential mates after just 30 seconds while only one in five men decided so quickly – so men, be aware that you may not have long to impress your date.

Wiseman also offered a piece of advice – steer clear of talking about films. During the experiment the researchers found discussing films only led to arguments. No one wanted to meet up afterwards, mainly because they'd disagreed about the best types of film. When the conversation turned to travel, however, people became far more enthusiastic and that subject ended in far more dates.

But don't get so obsessed by what you're meant to talk about and what you have to avoid that in the end you're just completely tongue-tied.

Whatever you say, make sure you smile when you say it. Smiling increases your chances of a positive response, regardless of what you utter.

Mark met Sarah, his partner of four years, at the second speed dating event he attended.

"I've only been to two speed dating events, which were both well organised in comfortable venues. The first was a dud for me but it gave me experience of the format," says Mark.

"I found that it doesn't take long to discover the degree of physical and mental chemistry with the person you are talking to. I didn't find it hard to talk and listen about 'something' for three minutes either, although after about the 20th conversation or so you have to avoid repeating yourself.

"There were a few people who I immediately knew were totally wrong for me and getting through three minutes in that situation can be tough. It also gets quite tiring and people start to blur, so making rudimentary notes is useful. Overall, the format is very good as you would need to go to a lot of parties to meet 20-plus similarly aged people who are interested in a relationship, of whatever type.

"I knew immediately after speaking to my partner-to-be something was afoot, and was hoping she'd ticked my box on the organisers' website (and worrying that she hadn't) so we could get in touch with each other. But she did and, over four years later, we remain immensely in love with each other."

CHAPTER 4

SINGLES HOLIDAYS

Going on holiday is hard when you're single. The thought of going to a place you don't know, finding things to do all day and then eating alone in restaurants at night is enough to put most people off.

There's nothing really quite like holidays to emphasise your single status. Brochures are full of pictures of happy couples strolling hand in hand along beautiful beaches, or of families playing in pools. And if you're looking for a partner it can be hard to admit that you're not going to be one of those people this summer.

But single people need holidays too!

So how do you approach it if most of your friends are in

relationships and have planned their summer trip with their partner or family?

You've probably found there are fewer invitations to join in with other people on holiday if you're not in a relationship – couples do like to go away with other couples unless there is a big group of people going.

So perhaps a singles holiday might be the answer. But what are they really like? And will you end up spending a week in a grotty hotel with a bunch of desperate people who can't hold a conversation?

In short – no.

Going on a singles holiday might not be the way to meet the next love of your life but it's a great way to have a break from your routine, meet new people and boost your self-confidence at a time when it is probably flagging a little.

> *"It was the most wonderful fun. We really gelled together as a group. I think by definition people going on holidays like that are fairly outgoing types. You've got to have a certain amount of confidence to go in the first place."*
> Colette, 56, who went on a singles holiday to
> Austria

The expert's view

You'll have fun and that, says Tony Knight of Solos Holidays, is the point.

"People have this fearful image of what other people are going to be like. They think it's going to be full of weirdos or desperate people," says Knight.

"The vast majority of people who travel with us are going away because they enjoy the company of other people and want to share experiences with other people. A lot of them have been divorced or lost their partner, and they have then lost contact with friends and are completely stranded."

Charlotte *went to Skyros, which is an alternative activity holiday centre on a Greek island where they run yoga classes, writing courses and so on.* "It was a beautiful place but there were plenty of women and only two, very weird men. Still, I met one of my now best friends there so it was well worth it despite the weird men and the oppressive therapy culture."

Colette *said her holiday had been a great way to reinvigorate herself as a single person.* "As a means of learning to relate to people as a single person again, I would definitely recommend it."

"They are a great way to have a holiday – you learn how to talk to people. Something I say a lot to people who are nervous is that it's a great way of getting some of your confidence back," says Jayne, who has been separated from her husband for several years and admits to having felt pretty lonely afterwards. "Last year I spent two weekends out of every four away all over the country. I really have not looked back."

It's likely there will be more women than men if you go on an organised singles trip, which obviously gives you better odds of finding a girlfriend than a new man – single men, take note.

The expert's view

Tony Knight says Solo Holidays get roughly three women to every man on their trips. So by the law of numbers, you may be more likely to meet the woman of your dreams.

"After the first holiday I went on I got an email six months later from a man saying he was going to marry a lady who was on that holiday. But that's very infrequent.

"You shouldn't go with that aim. All the other singles holiday companies would say the same thing. If you turn up and on the day you don't fancy anyone, you're going to be really miserable for the rest of the holiday."

So what sort of people go on these holidays? Are they going to be a bunch of sad, desperate weirdos who have no friends of their own? Probably not.

Some people travel alone because they have recently experienced a relationship breakdown and want to get away to have a break and cheer themselves up.

Others do it because none of their friends at home enjoys the same type of travelling – or maybe they can't get time off work, or have children to look after.

We all know how hard it can be to find friends who want to go to the same place, at the same time, and pay the same cost for a holiday – and often it's just not possible. Going on your own means you can choose exactly the type of holiday you want.

"Now that I've enjoyed the freedom of singles holidays I'm not sure I'd go away with a friend. It's a selfish thing but hey, I'm single.

"There's a freedom in going on holiday and not really having to think about anyone else. You can do what you want. But there's the security of having a group around you, not having to travel on your own, or eat on your own in particular." Jayne, *who has been on eight holidays with Solos over the last three years*

Another misconception of singles holidays is that you will be herded around like sheep by an over-enthusiastic tour rep and will be forced to join in with party games and group activities. But this is really quite far from the truth. In fact you probably have more opportunity to do exactly what you want on a singles holiday than when you go away with friends.

"With Solos you can dip in and out of the group as much as you want really – you can take yourself off and nobody will mind. Particularly with the big groups, two or three people will go off for the day to the town or to the hills. We don't all spend every minute of every day together.

Jayne explains: *"There's this myth that singles are Billy-no-mates or have two heads, but most of us aren't, we have just found ourselves on our own. Most of us have been married and are now divorced or widowed."*

Sue *says she didn't meet a man on the holiday she went on. "But it was great fun and I'd definitely do it again. I went with a girl friend and they were mostly women on the holiday, but it was still good."*

Another concern is age. How old will your travelling companions be and as an enthusiastic 45 year old are you going to be stuck on a coach with a group of rather tired 70 year olds? Not at all.

The biggest age band is from around 40 to 65 on most of these holidays and some companies specify age ranges for certain trips. But you are likely to find when you get there that the age doesn't really matter as much as you might think. Everyone is there to have a good time and it doesn't matter whether the person who makes you laugh over dinner is 40 or 50.

> *"My first singles holiday was lovely. I found it a completely liberating experience to go on holiday by myself without a partner. I was the youngest there and there were 21 of us – 18 women and three guys. That's the only holiday I've had where there has been that kind of ratio – on all the other ones it's been about 50:50 men and women. The mix makes for a really fun holiday with no pressure."* Jayne

One of the problems of going on a singles holiday with the aim of meeting a potential partner is that if you do meet someone, the chances of their living close enough to you to sustain a relationship when you get back home are pretty slim.

> *"I still think meeting people through friends is the best idea. I've gone on small group trips geared at singles, so you don't pay the single supplement, and I've made really good friends on those trips. But it would have to be*

pretty spectacular for you to say I'm going to start up a long-distance relationship with someone I just met and he lives 12 hours away by plane." Stephanie

But there are local organisations that run holidays, as well as weekends away and activity breaks. Cruising is a very popular one for singles – even Stelios of easyJet fame has got in on the act with his 'easyCruises' which tour the Aegean Sea. You can join his ship for a short break of a few nights or a full two-week holiday and the cruise is aimed at the young traveller market – a world away from the traditional cruise market.

The expert's view

"A cruise offers all the ingredients anybody could want from a holiday – it works far better than one stop destinations. We've just come back from a cruise to Rome, Sardinia and Monte Carlo and it was fantastic. On two of our holidays people have met partners – one on a cruise and one on a beach holiday in Corfu. This time one person who came with us met somebody on the last day of the holiday who wasn't in our group – so we'll see what happens," said Helen Ashford of Amité, a singles social group based in the South West.

Skiing is another activity that works really well for singles. The combination of having an energetic activity that you do with others from the group during the day, and eating a communal meal in a chalet in the evening, is a perfect recipe for getting to know your fellow holidaymakers and making you feel at ease travelling on your own. Within a day you probably won't feel that you came on holiday alone and there's nothing like a long chair lift ride to help get to know other people.

"I've done a couple of singles skiing holidays and it works really well. Not many of my friends ski and it's often hard for us to get a week off work at the same time. I've really enjoyed these trips – all the people who go are good fun, most of them are around my age and we all seem to get on really well. And yes, I have met some very nice women. I went out with one girl I met on the first trip for a few weeks after we got back but it didn't last. However, I've not been put off and I'll definitely do it again." Pete

If you're not quite energetic enough for skiing then you can join groups for walking, cycling or yoga holidays, visit ancient sites, try Pilates or learn how to sail. Learning a new skill while on holiday is also a great way to make you feel as though you've really achieved something – even if you don't come home with the woman or man of your dreams.

There is a list of holiday and event companies on the publisher's website (details at the back of the book) so why not give something a go this year? It could change your life.

Colette had been widowed for over six years and was 56 when she met Barry on a singles holiday. She hadn't dated since 1971. This is her story.

"I go to France almost every year on holiday and in 2005 I decided I'd like to do something a bit different.

Someone had recommended Travelsphere. They do a brochure called Just You and I saw this holiday in Austria right at the end of August. I'm not very adventurous really and I didn't fancy going anywhere I didn't speak the language at all so this seemed just right.

I had no thoughts whatsoever about meeting anyone on it but I had thought for about a year that it would be nice if it happened and I was open to the possibility.

I remember flying out – getting off the plane and on the coach and thinking 'Oh my God, what a boring looking lot of people'. Nothing could be further from the truth.

There were 18 women and five men from their mid 30s to 82 and it was just the most wonderful fun.

I stayed at the hotel on the Sunday and the others went

on an excursion. I went into the steam room in the afternoon and this chap came in and we chatted a bit. As I left I asked him if he was with the travel group and he said yes, he was."

In the first couple of days some of the group had noticed one woman who had already set her sights on Barry. She asked him out for walk one evening after dinner and, panic-stricken, he asked Colette to join them. The other woman was none too pleased.

"I noticed that he had such a lovely sexy voice. He flirted with me outrageously all week – that was the lovely thing, he was such a flirt.

It took me back to being in my teens again. I remember giggling a lot and it was tremendous fun. He was a real gent, and absolutely lovely.

At the end of the holiday he said I'm going to give you my address and number and I'd really like to hear from you. I said it wouldn't be for a week as I had to go back to work and sort myself out.

I was a gibbering wreck – it was such a bombshell that this was happening to me. I'd been on my own for $6^1/_2$ years since Peter died, and I'd started going out with him in 1971. It was 34 years since I'd had anything like this going on in my life. I was 56 and Barry was 60.

We got to Heathrow and he stayed with me. He got my hand luggage off the plane, he got one trolley and put both our cases on it. He waited with me until my bus came and put my luggage on the bus and waved me off. I had texted him before I left Heathrow.

He came to stay with me for the weekend two weeks after we got back. It was incredibly intense and very romantic.

What's so enjoyable about the whole thing is it's been so incredibly easy. It's so much simpler when you get to our age because when you're in your 20s they (potential partners) have to tick so many boxes. In your 40s or 50s all that is dealt with, all you're looking for is someone who makes you happy. That's the only box you have to tick.

I had been quite clear in my mind that anyone I met had to have been widowed or to have known Peter, but Barry seems to understand perfectly. He says how can you stop loving someone just because they've died?"

CHAPTER 5

THE SOCIAL CLUB SCENE

One of the ways of meeting new people when your social life is stuck in the doldrums is to join a social club.

There are many groups operating across the country which organise events and activities. The idea is that you pick events that interest you and by going along you are guaranteed to meet other people who share the same interests.

Most of these groups are not dating organisations – they simply organise the events, invite all their members and it's up to the members themselves to decide how much or how little they want to join in. If they come along to events, they can decide for themselves who they like and want to get to know better.

It's probably safe to say that most adults who are single and who have made the effort to join a group like this are actively looking for ways to improve their social lives and probably wouldn't be averse to meeting members of the opposite sex who they find attractive. Organisers say that members often meet and fall in love at their events.

One of the problems, however, is that there is still a bit of a stigma around 'joining a group'. Some people think that if you're not funny or popular enough to have a social life of your own and have to rely on someone else to organise it for you, then you must be a bit sad.

Simply not true, say the organisers and many of the people who go along to such events.

"When I split up with my husband I lost nearly all my friends. We had socialised more and more with his friends over the years and when we broke up it was really awkward for everyone. They're all still married and I just didn't fit in any more. The reason I come along to events like these is so that I can have a social life – I'd rather do this than sit in on my own every night." Kathy, in her late 40s

I heard this time and time again from many people who you would consider sensible, intelligent, fun adults but who have been through a relationship breakdown.

When you get divorced, your social life is likely to change. Either friends will side with one party or the other in the divorce, or you just won't feel like spending all your time with couples, so you will then seek out a different social life with people who are single.

Kathy, and others, admit that there is something disappointing about going out with a group of people you don't know very well, because you don't have a group of your own friends to go out with – but like all these things, if you go often enough it's likely that those people will become new friends and with each event you attend you'll have more fun.

"This is a really good way for women of my age to have a social life – I'm not about to go down the pub on my own when I want to get out of the house. But let's be honest, none of us would choose to do this rather than go out with a group of our own friends." Kathy

The expert's view

Anne Stringer runs RSVP Introductions, a service that runs social events and also does traditional 'matchmaking' in the Midlands, Essex and London.

"Sometimes people join as a social member first to dip their toe in the water and get a feel for what it's like being back out there. It's very difficult having been in a couple for a long period of time to be thrust out there as a single person. After a little while some will say they're ready to do introductions.

"I think when people come to us they are on a journey. We work with them wherever they are in that process. Sometimes people have just got to get used to seeing new people and going out again."

Stringer says she has often seen a member getting together with someone else they've met at one of the social events who she and her team would never have put together for an introduction. "You just can't beat the chemistry at the end of the day."

One of the problems that most social organisers face, but are reluctant to admit to, is that it's always easier to get women to come along to events than men. Women, generally, are willing to join in. They're prepared to admit that they're single, they'd like to meet new people and that they want to widen their social circle.

Men, on the other hand, just don't do these things. It's

easier for them to go to the local pub on their own and chat to people they know there, or they'll play football or golf with their mates once or twice a week and have a few drinks afterwards. That combined with work is usually enough to keep them busy and joining organised social events is probably something most men have never thought of.

Men are also extremely unlikely to admit to a friend that they want to go to a singles event, and wouldn't dream of taking a friend along if they did. Women will ask a girlfriend to keep them company if they don't want to turn up to something on their own, but men would rather not go than ask a friend to join them.

"I went to one event where you could only go if you took a single friend of the opposite sex and it was really good. We all have friends that we don't fancy, but they'd make a great partner for someone else." Fiona, who persuaded a good friend to go with her

So the chances are, when you go to organised social events, there are going to be more women than men in attendance, and the women will be of a generally higher calibre than the men – better looking and quite possibly better educated.

"I went to an organised dinner party which was in theory a great idea but all the men were unspeakable. One, the ugliest man I had ever seen, told me 'Man's love is of man's life a thing apart, 'tis woman's whole existence' – a quote from Byron which made him a) a pretentious twit and b) sadly misguided since he was desperate and I gladly went home alone." The rather off-putting experience of Louise, 39

However it's not all bad. If you want to improve your social life, get out more and make some new friends, then these groups are a great way of doing just that. You may not meet anyone who takes your breath away, but you will make new friends and just by doing that you have livened up your social life and are more likely to meet more new people and potentially a new partner.

The expert's view

Helen Ashford runs a social group, Amité, for single people over 30 in Devon. It is not a dating organisation and the group makes no attempt to attract even numbers of men and women to its events. It simply offers a packed programme of social events that single people can go to – from dinners, to pub lunches, country walks to picnics. You go along to something that takes your fancy, and the chances are you'll meet other people with similar inter-ests. If you don't meet the new love of your life, you'll cer-tainly make friends and that in turn boosts your confi-dence and can resurrect a suffering social life.

"I believe that 99 per cent of single people at 40 don't choose to be single. Everybody has a story to tell, and every one is worse than the last. We don't discuss the past – life is serious enough without having a serious social life," says Helen.

"I can't count how many people have met through me. Amité's primary aim is to bring single people together, but not just to expand their social life – it is a great way to meet new people, make new friends or even meet someone special! It really is the best way to meet peo-ple."

Amité has seen many couples get together over the years and Helen knows of three engagements so far this year. But she doesn't give much credence to the idea of match-making. "Nobody knows what that very special ingredi-ent is, called chemistry, which can only happen when two people meet."

Interestingly, one of the issues Anne Stringer raises is that for many people, walking into a social event of a group of people can be much harder than going on a blind date with a stranger. For many it's just too difficult to walk into a pub and say "Hello, I'm new and I'd like to join in" – or words to that effect.

People who have impressive careers, who deal with clients or customers or patients on a daily basis, who can cold-call people, sell things and do presentations to chief executives, still cannot bring themselves to go along to a singles party or social evening.

"Certain people are intimidated by coming into a group of people. They'll do the one to one thing, but not the events," Anne says.

However one thing most people – experts and members alike – agree on is that once you've taken the plunge and joined a social group like this, you have already taken a major step towards changing the patterns that you have got into with your social life.

The expert's view

"Everybody in this life has something to offer, whether they're nice to say Hi to, to share a cup of coffee with, or more. Joining a group like Amité is the most natural step to take – you just meet nice people. When you start a new job and you walk in there everybody seems so scary. It takes time, but within a week or two you feel comfortable – people don't look strange any more. This is no different," *Helen, of Amité*

"Having made a conscious decision to join an agency you're in a different frame of mind. You have opened yourself up to meeting a partner," *Anne, of RSVP Introductions*

It's worth pointing out that some social and activity groups like Spice, which organises events and outdoor activities across the UK, are not aimed specifically at singles and welcome couples as well. That doesn't mean you will have any less fun if you want to join in events like white water rafting, rock climbing or hill walking, but if you are joining with the express intent of meeting a future partner you may find it frustrating if you end up attending events with couples and people who are already attached.

Jon originally met his wife Lou through a singles social group three years ago. They now live together and are planning to get married.

"I'd been divorced for a few years and found that my social life consisted of going to the pub to watch a match with my mates, hanging out at my sister's house with her family or occasionally going to a party where everyone else seemed to be in couples.

I just felt like I was missing out a bit on life – and getting older fast. I'd seen several ads for the social group in the local newspaper so one day I just thought I'd give it a go. They had organised a walk on the hills not far from me and it's something I hadn't done for years so I decided to go along. It was a good day out – fresh air, good exercise and the people were nice. I didn't meet anyone I would have asked on a date, but I had some interesting conversations and it felt good to be meeting new people and talking about different stuff.

I decided to go along to some other events and some were good, some not so much fun, but then after about six months I met Lou. We got chatting at first and found we shared the same sense of humour – it was ages since I'd really laughed and we both enjoyed each other's company. We agreed to attend another event a couple of weeks later, it was a meal in a pub, and we found we spent the whole evening talking to each other.

After that it was just really natural. We met up on our own and both realised we didn't want to attend the social group events any more. We've kept in touch with a couple of the people we met at the group, but now I find my social life is beginning to widen out again. I've met all Lou's family and her friends and she's met mine.

It's sad to admit, but when you're in a couple you're definitely more 'socially acceptable' and you do get more invitations. That's just life I suppose. Meeting Lou has transformed my life – and I never honestly thought it would happen through that sort of group. I am genuinely happy. She's great fun, she makes me laugh. I love her to bits."

CHAPTER 6

THE OLD-FASHIONED METHOD

There are so many dating tricks out there that you might easily be forgiven for thinking the only way to meet someone these days is to spend your time glued to an internet connection or to go on a string of embarrassing and unproductive blind dates.

But that's not necessarily the case. For many people the old methods are the best, and by that I mean meeting a future partner through friends.

Lorraine had been widowed 18 months when her friend Sally invited her to a party. Also invited was a colleague of Sally's husband who was single. Sally was pretty sure they would get on and made sure he was properly introduced to her at the party. After a rather bumpy start their relationship eventually took off and less than two years later they were married in a beautiful wedding, with her young children as bridesmaids.

Susan had been single for a long time and was beginning to think she'd never meet Mr Right, despite dozens of night classes and several sports clubs. One night she was in the pub with friends when she spilt a drink on a stranger on the way back from the bar. Four years later they are living together with their son and baby daughter.

Paul had gone abroad as a volunteer after the break-up of a long-term relationship so he could get a new perspective on life and ring some changes. A couple of years later, back in the UK, he joined a group for returning volunteers as a way of making some new friends in the city where he now lived. He met Julie and they became friends. Several years later they are living together and hope to start a family.

None of these people were expecting to meet future life partners where they did, but their stories prove that you can meet your match anywhere, at any time. And if you're introduced by good mutual friends, there's a strong likelihood that you will have something in common and like each other.

If nothing else, having mutual friends gives you a rich conversation topic to get started on when you're first left on your own.

One rather jaded internet dater put it like this in his profile:

"Even if you do meet someone who ticks enough of your impossible quota of boxes, the first time that person does anything you're slightly unsure of, they're dumped faster than you can say 'You look a lot slimmer in your picture' because you know nothing about them which makes it so easy to say goodbye. For a relationship to survive those first of many doubts there has to be a level of clearance from someone you or your friends know.

"We all need an introduction from a mate who says they're OK, otherwise you'll find fault in no time. Stop working so hard and get down the pub with your mates. Take a few days out to work out how to get that part of your life back that you loved so much before you had the mortgage/kids/STD/cellulite. Go and meet someone in the real world."

He's blunt, but he has a point. Someone you know in common who can vouch for your potential date goes a long way to give you confidence in a person you have never met before and know absolutely nothing about.

So if you're looking for a new partner, how can you get your friends on board? Here are some nuggets of advice that may sound obvious but they're worth thinking about. After all, you may not be doing everything you can to help yourself.

MAKE SURE YOUR FRIENDS KNOW YOU WANT TO MEET SOMEONE

It's easy to think everyone knows you're looking, but you'd be surprised how many people aren't aware that you're serious about meeting a new partner. If they don't know, they won't think to introduce you to the colleague, friend, neighbour or relative they know who is also single. If they do know, then the next time they come across someone eligible, they'll think of you (hopefully).

ACCEPT EVERY INVITATION YOU ARE OFFERED

OK, so the village Harvest Supper or morning coffee at a friend's house may not sound like the stuff of romance, but socialising with friends is the best way to get out, practise having fun and make interesting conversation – and is also a good way to let it be known you're on the lookout for someone special. If you're chatting to a group of friends, it's perfectly acceptable to suggest they do a spot of matchmaking. You just never know who might come up with a gem of an idea. We surveyed 90 people for this book and only three of them said they wanted to keep their dating private and hated the idea of being set up by their friends.

INVITE PEOPLE TO YOUR HOUSE OR TO GO OUT WITH YOU

Don't just sit and wait for the invites to come to you. If you ask people to come to dinner at your house, to the cinema or for a coffee then the chances are they'll repay your hospitality. And when you do get invited back, you may well widen your circle of friends by meeting people there who you didn't know before.

GET A DOG

If it's possible for you to own a dog it could help you find a partner. Getting out every day and going for walks will help you get fit, feel better and look better. But not only that, it's also a great way to meet other dog walkers. Remember the good-looking blond guy who appeared in the BBC's Castaway series on the Scottish island of Taransay with his black labrador Inca? Well Ben Fogle met his wife Marina while out walking Inca in Hyde Park, when she took a shine to Marina's own labrador.

JOIN A CLASS

This, of course, is the old staple of agony aunt columns. "Join a night class my dear," was the mantra they used to solve a multitude of problems. But it's not so daft – just be aware of the kind of class you join.

If you go to a needlework or pottery class, the chances are quite high you will meet a lot of women, which is great for the blokes, but perhaps not so good if you're looking for a husband. You could try car maintenance, basic DIY or woodwork, but beware there will quite possibly be many other women there who've had the same idea. And you'll be meeting mechanics.

Languages are perhaps a better idea. Conversation is a big part of foreign language night classes, giving you the perfect excuse to chat up fellow students. I heard of a woman who is now living with someone she met at a French class. When told to ask her partner something she asked him if he'd like to go out for a beer. The rest, as they say, is history.

Active pursuits like swimming, sailing and running are a good bet. All of these clubs have a really good mix of men and women – and people who are keen to look after themselves to boot. If you don't do any of these sports then it's never too late to start. Tennis clubs are very social and often have evenings where everyone mixes – a good way to meet new faces. Gyms, however, are not the best place to meet new people. When was the last time you actually spoke to the person on the running machine next to you?

Dance classes are more sociable. Do something like salsa and you'll be literally thrust into the arms of a stranger in order to take part. Usually more women than men here, so a good one for the guys. Salsa classes are often followed by a club night so if you do meet someone you like it's easy to dance the night away.

Find out what's on in your local area by going to hotcourses.com or ring up your local further education college and ask for a brochure. You can usually start adult education classes in September, January and April.

None of this is rocket science. It's more to do with expanding your circle of friends, getting out, meeting people and generally being open to any opportunities.

You may have found your life situation changing because of divorce or bereavement. Being single again after years of being part of a couple is scary and bewildering but remember, you're not the only one this is happening to. Even if it feels like the rest of the world is part of a couple, people all around you have changing lives too.

I'm not saying you should sit around and wait until your friends get divorced or lose a partner so you can snap them up. But I am saying that the couple you met at a party a couple of years ago, who live down the road from your friend, may have hit a rough patch in the intervening period and you may meet again and find that you're both now in the same single boat.

"You have to use your existing network – and there's no shame about it. If you're embarrassed to admit you'd like to meet someone then you're missing an opportunity." Claire Gillbanks, who runs Meet at Last, a dating and events company in London

It seems that people tend to socialise with others in a similar situation, so young couples without kids go out and have a great time together, people with babies and young children stick together because they're all in the same boat of tiredness and having to cart around a ton of equipment to go anywhere. When you split up with a partner, or are bereaved, suddenly you've jumped into a different boat and all your friends are still sailing along on the same path.

This is what makes it difficult and it takes time to find other people who are in similar circumstances to your own. Once you do, it makes it easier to start going out again and socialising.

"I hardly know any married people at all any more," says Bill, who lives only a few miles away from me. While I'm surrounded by married couples, he feels he's surrounded by single and divorced people. It could be an age thing – he's 10 years older than me. Maybe this is what happens, or it could be that he socialises as a single person and therefore meets other single people. They are out there, and once you start finding them you'd be surprised how many there are.

"I can walk around Waitrose and I can spot a divorced woman – and it's not just about what's in her basket. They have an aura around them. It has helped me do my predatory male thing. You can also drop a couple of questions that can tell you straight away, like 'What do you do at the weekend?' Obviously 'Every other weekend I have my kids' is a dead giveaway." Philip

Many older widowed people meet other widows and find they get a second chance at happiness when they least expected it. But you will only meet those people if you are active, sociable and get out and about.

In our survey 44% of respondents said their friends had never come up with anyone they could meet. However a whopping 98% said they wanted their friends to help them find a partner.

A television series called *Arrange Me a Marriage* has caught on to this and is trying to bring the Indian methods of using your family's social network to find a suitable partner to the white community. Many people think arranged marriages are archaic and impersonal but they do make a certain amount of sense. Anyone who is connected to your own network is, to a certain extent, a known quantity – they're not just a random stranger you've met in a bar or through a website. Because you have a connection, however tenuous, you have some common ground, something to talk about, a way of breaking the ice.

So why do we find it so difficult to help our friends find a partner?

Many friends have said to me, "I know a couple of single men but I'd never dream of trying to pair you off with them, they're all useless/mad/dangerous/bad news" – insert your own negative adjective.

Or worse, the friend who knew a very eligible single man and said to me, "Oh God, I'd *hate* you to think I was trying to set you up!"

Why? And how do they know that I wouldn't fall head over heels for one of their useless/crazy/dangerous friends?

The expert's view

Anne Stringer says: "You can't beat the chemistry at the end of the day. We do get people who meet at events who we would never have put together."

And she's a professional matchmaker. If she can't judge it right all the time, don't expect your friends to either.

So do yourself a favour. Have a party. Get a friend to join in so you can enjoy the preparation together. Invite all your single friends as well as the couple-friends you really like. Then tell everyone who's coming not to bring a bottle but to bring a single friend. Introduce people to each other, maybe even play a game, get people talking, break the ice. You could be very surprised what happens.

Jack had come out of a long relationship and put an ad in the Soulmates column of the Guardian newspaper. Suzanna was the second person he met and they were married earlier this year. This is their story.

"I thought I'd do something different so I based my ad on Sex and the City. Because you don't know what's going to happen neither of us thought to keep the ad, but it was something about not being Big, and looking for Carrie but with a better dress sense. All those ads are so lacking in imagination.

I had about 60 or 70 replies. Because I had so many replies I thought I'll call 10 and go on about seven or eight dates. Suzanna wasn't on the first list of 10 but I had a reserve list. I thought if any of them aren't in, I'll phone the reserves. I wasn't going to call her initially because she said she liked camping and I'd just come back from Alaska and had had a disastrous two-week camping trip which I just hated.

She was number 11 – luckily the person before didn't pick up the phone so I called Suzanna. I arranged to meet her on the next night.

They were all surprisingly normal. I really enjoyed the

whole process. I enjoyed having the evenings out and of all the people I thought I'd go out with, only one was a bit scary.

When I met Suzanna I wasn't fully over my last relationship. You find yourself single in your mid-30s and not expecting to be. I didn't fully appreciate what makes me happy so I wasn't fully committed for a year. Then we went a bit fast forward.

I completely recommend it – after all if it doesn't work you've only wasted half an hour of your time meeting up with someone. I did choose the Guardian deliberately – you're going to meet Guardian readers. I'd never put an ad in the Telegraph!"

Suzanna:

"I'd never done anything like this before. My flatmate encouraged me to do it. I had replied to one other ad – I was supposed to meet the guy but he didn't turn up. I thought he might have seen me and run away so I said I was only going to do it one more time. Then I replied to Jack's ad. I had to ring and listen to his message, then leave my details.

That was the first thing – when I phoned up I thought Jack had a really lovely voice. It was just the way he said he was and I thought he's the kind of person I want. I'd come out of a long-term relationship and had a brief relationship in the meantime but at that point you're just not meeting new people through friends any more.

The people doing this are often very normal people who just don't have the opportunities to meet people.

We both told our parents who thought it was quite amusing. There was no mention of if at the wedding. We didn't consciously try to hide it but didn't make a thing of it either.

A lot of people can't quite believe we met through the Guardian. We work in slightly related professions and could have met through work. In our first conversation Jack said he'd been for an interview with a company I knew quite well and we made a connection. When you reply to an ad you think it could be anyone, he could be a psycho, but as he knew people I knew I felt more confident.

I think the internet is a bit more scary. People can get away with a lot more and create a persona that's not true. But with this process you have to have a phone call straight away so it doesn't even go anywhere if that doesn't work. When you ring people up you do get a sense of who they are.

I would encourage friends to do it. We really have been
lucky. You're increasing your number of chances of
meeting the right people."

CHAPTER 7

DATING AS PARENTS

This chapter was going to be called 'dating with kids' but then I realised that no one, in their right mind, would go on a date with their kids. Well, not with mine, anyway.

I remember one day talking to someone who said she had a friend – a man – whose divorce had recently come through. He was finding it hard to meet women locally who interested him and said he was going to have to spread his net a bit wider.

We were going for lunch together and I rashly suggested she bring him along. Boy was I glad that she didn't take up my suggestion.

Child number one was grabbing the chips while child

number two cried because I forgot to buy her a lemonade. Then one of them fell in the mud and the other made a fuss because she didn't get pudding. Normal Sunday lunch in a pub really ... but would I want a potential date to see me dealing with this and trying to keep my cool? Certainly not.

Dating as a parent is a totally different ball game from dating as a single person without children – whether you're 25, 35, 45 or even 55. It doesn't really matter how old your children are, they still loom over your dating experiences and can make or break a relationship.

Let's look at the age groups and think about the implications. Age bands are approximate so your child and you may well fall into more than one category.

0–3 YEARS

You're tired all the time, you have broken nights and you've forgotten what it's like to go out without milk stains on your clothes. You possibly can't get into any of your posh party clothes because the last time you wore them was pre-pregnancy, and you're so absorbed with the overwhelming task of looking after tiny children on your own that you're not sure you can even hold a conversation about anything else. For fathers in this position you're probably pretty brain dead due to broken sleep, and you're aware that your fatherhood screams 'fertile' at any woman of a certain age who wants to become a mother, so you have to tread carefully if you don't want to produce even more offspring in the near future. And any woman who is not full of maternal urges is unlikely to find the thought of sharing alternate weekends with someone small and in nappies very appealing.

4-8 YEARS

This is possibly the age group that is least appealing to prospective dates. Your children can be wilful and stroppy and are likely to be reacting to whatever circumstances mean you're on your own as a parent. If their parents have split up they may be wary of new partners and clingy to the parent who cares for them most of the time. Bereaved children may well at this stage be desperate to replace the lost parent – potentially tricky for any hope of a casual relationship. To dates these children can be ever-present, still needing quite intense parenting yet not nearly as cute – or as easy to win over – as an 18 month old who's just learning to talk. Parents are tired, stressed, find it hard to get out in the evening and have their hands pretty much full with all the associated stuff that goes with young children – school runs, washing, cooking, playing and so on.

9-13 YEARS

Perhaps now is the time that children really don't want their parent to find a new relationship. They're old enough to know Mum or Dad was hurt by someone else, they may be aware of a recent relationship that hasn't worked out, they find the idea of a parent as a sexual being a tricky one to deal with. Their own hormones are also beginning to kick in and that's likely to have a serious effect on their ability to be rational. About anything – far less Mum or Dad dating.

14-18 YEARS

Get them on board at this age and you can be onto a good thing, though a teenager who is against the idea of Mum or Dad dating could be quite scary. Many a teenager has helped their parent write a profile for an online dating site and if they're fairly sorted about the reason their parents are on their own then they'll be pleased to think that Mum or Dad might have some fun and have someone else in their lives to look after them. Logic could also dictate that if a parent is falling in love they'll be a bit distracted and less likely to be on their kids' case all the time about what they're up to.

I'm sure every single parent has thought at some point that it might just be easier to give up dating before they even start.

One option is to wait until your children have all left home and then indulge yourself – but why should you? After all, a happy parent makes for a happy child and you shouldn't feel you have to put your whole life on hold because you have children. Thousands of parents are on their own and many of them go on to form happy, stable relationships with other people which bring real benefit to their children's lives.

PLAYING TWO PARTS

So, as a parent, how do you combine the two roles of dating grown-up and parent?

"I find it quite hard to summon up the energy for dating. My children are quite demanding and I am bringing them up alone so I don't often get a break. The thought of finding a babysitter, getting dressed up and getting out in the evening is quite daunting, let alone being confident that I'll have the energy to make interesting conversation

and have a laugh. The last thing I want to do is to go out and moan about my kids or be a bore about them. But on the other hand they are absolutely the most important thing in my life and it is vital for me that any man who shows an interest in me can understand that." Kate

"The main problem I found with having a child was that it tended to be my parents or in-laws babysitting and I didn't necessarily want to tell them every time I was going on a date. I felt that I'd lost the independence and privacy that I had when I was dating before, when I'd never have divulged such information. I tried to find other people to babysit so that I didn't have to tell them. By the age of two, Molly was able to tell her grandparents who was in Mummy's bed last night and I was always half expecting her to land me in it." Julie, who was widowed when her daughter was a baby

You do certainly feel that there is less privacy when dating as a parent and it can be strange when you have older children who are more aware of what's really going on.

"I have to come home to an 18 year old in the morning who knows exactly what I've been doing. How do you think that makes me feel?" says a friend of mine who recently began a new relationship.

DATING OTHER PARENTS

Does it work best if you date other parents or can it work if you meet someone who doesn't already have children?

Opinions differ and there's no right answer, but the truth is that parents have more understanding of what it's like to be a parent. They know how much you can love your own child. They know how tiring and demanding it can be. Any good parent will know how important your children will be to you and will expect them to come first in any major life decisions you make.

But sometimes even other parents can't quite get their heads round the fact that they're going to be playing second fiddle to a partner's child.

"I had been dating Steve for a while but then when there was the possibility that he might stay the night, my daughter Sarah was very uncomfortable about it. It was tricky because she didn't want to be here if he stayed but I didn't want to tell her to stay at someone else's. She wasn't happy even if he stayed on the sofa – she's 16 remember and as a young woman isn't used to there being a man around. It eventually felt like a bit of a power struggle between them and I had to think about who was

my greater priority, and you've guessed it, Sarah won out." Jan

Another problem with dating another parent is that you automatically have two sets of children to think about and the interaction between them can add extra pressure to a relationship.

"I think that it is extremely difficult dating when you have children as they are your priority and so there is bound to be some conflict. But I suppose if you had children that kept normal hours then you would have the evenings together – not a luxury that I had. In one relationship I had, my partner and daughter vied for my attention. I felt as if I was being pulled apart. It was a horrid feeling. He really could have been more mature but perhaps as he had limited time available I might have arranged more time alone." Jenny, who has dated on and off since Emma, who is now 18, was very young

If you're dating someone who has children you have to remember that you are the grown-up, not the child, and it's up to you to act like it. It's not very adult to be jealous of the relationship a parent has with their child, and if you can't handle that existing – and extremely important – relationship then you are not the right partner for them.

I dated a guy for a couple of months and we began by having a weird nocturnal relationship because I didn't want the children to know early on. I would go round to his house, eat dinner and stay for a while and then come creeping back in the dead of night, absolutely shattered and climb quietly into bed so the children wouldn't wake up (it's OK, I had a friend living with me so they weren't home alone). Eventually I got so exhausted that I decided we would have to see each other in daylight, which meant him meeting the children as they are always around in the evenings and at weekends. The second time he came to the house I opened the front door and he greeted me with a big smile and a friendly kiss. Little did I realise that the children were at the top of the stairs watching everything that was happening and no sooner had he stepped inside than one of them said: "Eugh, you kissed our Mummy! Does that mean you're going to marry her and be our new Daddy?"

As we drove off to dinner a bit later I said rather lamely: "No pressure … it's early days," but somehow it rang a bit hollow. I told him that in the fairy tales we were reading at the time the first kiss was always followed on the next page by the big white wedding, and unfortunately that was their reality (I could have thrown the Sleeping Beauty book straight in the bin). Needless to say the relationship was doomed and we broke up a few weeks later.

Sometimes, as a parent, it's hard not to resent your children when things go wrong and hard not to take out your frustrations if you've been badly let down by someone new in your life.

Children can't understand why Mummy is glowing and giggling one week and grumpy as hell the next. Learning to live with the two roles is quite a challenge for anyone.

More than half the parents (55%) who responded to our survey said being a parent made it much harder for them to find the time to date, 14% said their children were so horrible to anyone they brought home that dates don't want to come back, and 14% said their children were really against them dating.

However, on the positive side 18% of parents said their children would love them to do more dating.

> *"At first my children were really against it and thought it was terrible, crying to my friends and family. But now they've accepted it and insist on coming with us."* Claire

Kids can also be quite a good barometer of who is worth dating. After all, they know you pretty well and have some kind of instinct about what would make you happy.

> *"I have only introduced my children to two men I was dating. The first they grew to dislike with such a vehemence that as he was coming in the front door, they exited by the back door. In the event, they were right. On another occasion, a man came to take me out and met my son. En route to the concert, I received a text from my son saying 'He may be small, fat and bald but he looks well-heeled. Game on! Enjoy!'"* Annette

> Jenny *says it was hardest when Emma was 13. "She hated the retired brigadier that I found so she kept hiding his cards and deleting his number from my phone. She has always been very tactful and polite unless she decides that they are upsetting me. Then beware!"*

Even being a grandparent can have its drawbacks. Often you're expected to be ready and willing to babysit at a moment's notice and, if you're on your own, your grown-up children may well think they're doing you a favour by asking you, so you feel 'needed'. Perhaps you'd rather be needed in other ways though.

> *"I have two children and four grandchildren. My wife loved the kids and she loved having them here, but it's not*

my pleasure. I need to be out and about. I'm happy to have them for an hour or so but I don't want them all the time." Cliff

Simon, *47, says he would now only date another parent after difficult experiences with women who don't have children. "It makes it easier if the woman has had kids because they understand my situation as a single parent. My previous girlfriend hadn't had children and there were real issues between her and my son: they were both jealous of each other. He was jealous of her because she was encroaching on his time with me, and she was jealous of the closeness between him and me. She couldn't get her head round it.*

"We used to have rows and I'd say you can't possibly understand this. Then she would accuse me of having a go at her because she hadn't had kids."

Peter *also had a bad experience dating a childless woman in her 40s. "She seemed child friendly but when it really came down to it, she didn't realise what being a parent meant at all – and why should she?"*

You have to be honest with people about having children, otherwise a relationship is really going to go nowhere.

"The trouble with dating a guy with his own family is that the families get to know each other and then if the relationship fails, the children are moping because they have lost the rest of their family." Jenny

A friend of mine went out to a bar one night with a girlfriend and got chatted up. She was enjoying the attention and didn't want to tell him anything about her difficult situation – bereaved with two very young children. She said she was divorced and left it at that.

Then he asked her out and on their first date she had to admit that not only was she not divorced but she had two boys under five as well. It didn't make for an easy start to a relationship.

People do need to know what they're getting into. It's far better to say on an internet profile that you have two kids who you see every weekend, or a teenager who lives with you, than pretend they don't exist. If you attract people who aren't interested in children it's only going to lead to problems later on. After all, why would you want to date someone who wasn't interested in one of the most important aspects of your life?

Dating as a parent is certainly nothing to be ashamed of. There are thousands of parents looking for new relationships and many people who don't have children of their own who will be only too happy to play a role in bringing up yours.

Several internet sites cater specifically for parents, and some include profiles of people who don't have their own children but are happy to meet people who are already parents. The main UK-based sites are:

Kids No Object **www.kno.org.uk**
Parents Already **www.Parentsalready.com**
Dating for Parents **www.datingforparents.com**
Lone Parents **www.lone-parents.org.uk/dating.htm**

There are others aiming at the parent market, but many are international and as it's fairly hard to sort out babysitting when you're going into town, starting a relationship with someone in Manila or Michigan is probably going to be an even tougher nut to crack.

The expert's view

If you are looking for another parent to date, don't assume that it would be best to find someone who has children of the same age as yours. In fact, this can be the hardest combination to make work. Kids No Object explains:

"Many families have children that cover a wide age span, and co-exist quite happily. If your partner has children in an entirely different age group, this could work in your favour, as it may stop or reduce rivalry between the children of the two families. Older children will often warm quicker to much younger children and feel protective towards them. Similarly, younger children will look up to older children, and not feel that they have to compete with them."

"I think it depends on whether the children get on. I have had older stepchildren who liked playing with Emma when she was little. Perhaps different ages are easier – there's less competition and more individual roles in the new set up." Jenny

INTRODUCING THE KIDS

But before you have to worry about whether the kids will get on with each other, when do you actually introduce your kids to your new partner? Or taken the other way, when do you introduce your new partner to your children?

Should you let them meet right at the beginning so that your partner can see the people that he/she might potentially become quite involved with? Or should you wait until your relationship is pretty solid so that you feel more confident?

Is it fairer to your children to meet a new partner early on so they can have some say in whether they want this person to become part of their family network? Or is it better for them to wait until he or she is a serious part of the deal before being introduced?

It's probably best to wait at least until you think this person is going to be significant in your life. It's unsettling and unfair for children to introduce them to a string of boyfriends or girlfriends – and if you do they are less likely to want to become attached to your new partners.

When you do make the introduction, try and plan it around something the kids like doing – go to the park together, go bowling or to the cinema. It will help the children if they are doing something they enjoy and will reinforce positive feelings towards the new partner.

Your children, whatever their age, are bound to be jealous of the new person in your life and may feel excluded. They may also want to spend more time with their other parent. It takes time for children to adjust to a new relationship and just because you've fallen in love with this person it doesn't necessarily mean your children will too.

"I have always led a very open life so Emma always knew any man early on. So I wasn't introducing her to someone that I already had a relationship with. She has always been very tactful and polite unless she decides that they are upsetting me." Jenny

Julie *said she went on a few lunch dates with her two-year-old daughter in attendance. "Luckily she's pretty well behaved in a restaurant as long as she's got something unhealthy in front of her to eat. Actually I think it made the dates easier, less formal. Children do funny things, which breaks the ice a bit. She was a good distraction or conversation topic when it was needed. And actually looking back it was a good idea – it was good they knew from the start what my life could be like and whether that was for them or not. If they couldn't cope with Molly being around then there wasn't going to be much hope for the relationship anyway, so it was good to see what they were like in that situation.*

"I remember, whilst on a second date, looking across at Molly in a restaurant, covered in chocolate cake and a fair sprinkling on the floor, feeling slightly embarrassed,

and saying to my date (who is now my partner) 'this was your idea by the way' to which he said, 'Yes, because she's part of the package'. He thought she was very well behaved and wasn't at all embarrassed. That was a great relief."

Dating another parent, if all goes well, can ultimately lead to a situation where both sets of children have to learn to accept each other as part of their family network. Having children of the same age can cause more rivalry because they feel more direct competition for parents' attention, and if they don't naturally bond with each other you could be in for a rough ride.

It can be extremely hard for children to welcome strangers into their home, or move into a stranger's home, and to treat them as family. It needs patience and understanding on the part of the parent and it's important to look at the situation from the child's point of view.

Giving all the children in the new set-up plenty of love and affection is important, as is praising them for sharing and co-operating with each other.

Remember that children come together with different expectations, family habits and rules. They may well be jealous over their possessions, their space and their parents.

The expert's view

As the website www.raisingkids.co.uk says: "You chose your partner. Your children did not choose your partner's kids. If you've ever shared a house, remember how difficult flatmates can be? And you usually have some say in choosing a flatmate."

But forming step-families is a whole other book ... so we'll move on.

Rachel was the second person Tony met through a single parents' internet dating site. She had one son and he was caring for four children. They were married in December 2006, 20 months later. This is their story.

"Rachel was the second person I met. She emailed me first. I thought I liked the sound of her, and I emailed her back. After about two weeks we began to talk a lot by email, we started going downstairs at night to write to each other and we arranged to speak on the phone. The first phone call lasted four hours and we've never gone a day without phoning each other since.

"We'd both come to the decision that we loved each other even though we'd never met face to face. There was never any doubt in my mind that I wouldn't fancy her. It hadn't crossed my mind that we wouldn't hit it off, but I was prepared for her to pull up in the car, see me and drive off. We'd spoken for so long and we had such a chemistry.

"We emailed for a month before we spoke. Then we met five days later. Rachel moved in seven months later – it was very quick, but we all clicked, it seemed natural. We found that we couldn't live apart.

"My children love her to bits. It's hard work because she's gone from having one child to having five so it's quite tough. But they had a lot of bad experiences with their mum who was so different from Rachel. They love her – she's done all the things a mum should do with my 13 year old daughter.

"Rachel's son Joe has also benefited from living with a man who loves him, treats him like his own son, and who really loves his mum."

CHAPTER 8

THE FIRST DATE

So, somehow or other, you have got to the first date. It really doesn't matter how you got there – the next thing you have to do is to congratulate yourself. As we've seen, it can be quite a tortuous process to go from "I think it's time I started dating again" to "Let's meet on Thursday for a drink".

Before you go any further, do one of the following things:

◆ Indulge in a chocolate brownie with your afternoon cup of tea today.

◆ Sit down and read the paper/a good book/watch some TV *before* doing the washing up or hoovering.

◆ Go for a good walk or a swim instead of cooking dinner. A takeaway really won't harm the kids and they'll probably thank you for it.

Only after you've spoiled yourself a bit can you think about the date.

But why are you spoiling yourself now, you wonder? Well, the date may be fantastic and you may be about to meet someone who will become truly significant in your life. I hope you will.

But the chances are you'll have an enjoyable drink and decide that actually he/she wasn't really what you were looking for and you'll be back to the drawing board. In which case you'll probably feel a bit down and not much like celebrating. Which is why I think it's a great idea to celebrate the fact you've lined up a date beforehand, and then it doesn't matter which way it pans out.

Seriously though, the big day is finally arriving. You have two days to work out what you're going to wear, what you'll say, what to ask him/her ... all nerve-wracking stuff. But it doesn't have to be. Let's go through a first-date scenario one step at a time and see how simple it can be with a bit of planning.

WHEN AND WHERE TO MEET

There are lots of options for a date, but on a first date you really want to try and keep your meeting quite short. If you commit yourself to dinner then you're going to be stuck with each other for the whole evening, even if you find each other quite unpleasant. And it can be tricky finding an excuse to leave half-way through a meal. So plan to meet for a coffee or a drink earlier in the evening and say you have arranged to meet a friend afterwards, then you have the perfect excuse to leave after an hour.

You could either meet at a coffee shop in the morning, or a café or bar after work for a drink. There will be a more relaxed atmosphere in the early evening and you might find it more comfortable than meeting a stranger in the morning when the light is bright and it all feels a bit more business-like.

After work is a good time to meet – unless of course you have children, in which case anything between 4pm and 8pm is really out of the question. If you have school-age children I'd suggest you arrange to meet during the day, as you can take your time to get ready, you won't have to arrange a babysitter and you won't have to explain to your nosy children where you are going, who you are meeting and what time you'll be back. You can do it all in secret, which adds to the fun.

If you don't have children then arrange to meet in a friendly, social venue after work and line something up with a friend for afterwards if you can, so you can head off confidently, knowing you're meeting up with someone you like. Then if the date is a success you can tell them all about it when you're at your most excited, and if it's a disaster you can laugh it off and have a good evening anyway.

Keep it public

Always arrange a first date in a busy, public place. Don't be intimidated by the thought that other people will be watching you and will know you're on a date. No one will know it's a first date and no one else will be interested in what you're up to anyway. But for safety's sake you should always meet someone you don't know in public. (There's more about safety in the next chapter.)

What to wear

Working out what to wear on a date is probably the hardest part of the whole experience, especially if you have never met before and you don't know what kind of clothes your date wears.

Obviously it will depend a bit on where and at what time you're meeting. If you're going for coffee in the morning you will probably want to dress slightly differently than if you're meeting in a trendy bar in the evening. But some golden rules still apply.

Don't go over the top. For women, the best advice is 'tits or legs' but not both. So if you want to wear a slightly sexy top that shows off your beautiful bosom, then team it with trousers or a longish skirt, and if you have a great pair of legs then show them off but keep your top half pretty well covered. Showing too much flesh up top and down below will just make you look tarty.

Put some make-up on and do your hair nicely. You don't have to spend £50 at the hairdressers or buy anything new but you should aim to look clean and as if you've made an effort. My mother would say clean and neat, but this isn't a job interview – don't change your natural style and if you *live* in your jeans then wear them, but wear a clean pair and think about putting on a nice top. There's absolutely no point in going on a date dressed up like a different person. If you meet again your date will soon discover the real you, and it's far better for them to get a good idea of who you are on the first date than a few weeks later when you have let the mask slip.

> Peter *arranged to meet a woman for a walk in the country after chatting online for a while.* "She'd told me she was into the outdoors, which is really important to me, and she turned up in a pair of high heels! I was really cross. She obviously didn't have a clue and in the end we had to go and have a drink in the pub. I didn't see her again."

Also remember that you'll be a bit nervous on the first date and dressing in a way that makes you feel comfortable is far more important than dressing to impress. This is about confidence – if you feel relaxed and confident that will come across in the way you talk and behave. But if you feel ill at ease in new clothes that don't fit, you won't be able to relax and have an easy conversation.

This all applies to men as well. I'd say there's nothing wrong with jeans, but if you're older you will probably want to dress up a little smarter. Don't feel obliged to wear a tie, but remember a woman will notice if you've shaved and washed your hair – and got clean shoes on.

In fact it's said that some women will judge a man on his shoes *alone*, so be warned. Little things, but they speak volumes and there are few women around who'll want to date a man who obviously can't look after himself.

CONVERSATION

So, you're dressed, you know where you're going – the next thing is what on earth are you going to say to him?

Making conversation with a stranger needn't be difficult and you shouldn't be nervous of doing so. By the time you've arranged a first date it's probably safe to assume you know a little about each other. Even if you've been set up by friends on a blind date and don't know much about each other at all, at least you have those friends in common and that's probably as good a place as any to start your conversation.

The most important thing to remember is to listen as well as talk. Men, particularly, are liable to talk a great deal about themselves and not be so good at asking questions – or worse, they ask questions but don't listen to the answers. So make a mental note: your date will want you to be interested in them, so show you are interested.

"I chatted to a man online for a couple of weeks and we'd exchanged lots of good emails. He seemed to be interested in the same things as me, he had a son so I felt relaxed talking about my children, and it was all looking very promising. Then one Monday morning he emailed me his phone number and said he didn't feel much like working – we both work from home. So I called him and we chatted for at least an hour. He seemed friendly though it did cross my mind that he liked to talk about himself quite a bit. Anyway, people can be funny on the phone so when he suggested a coffee I agreed and we met up a few days later.

"We sat down and I have to admit there was no immediate chemistry on my part, though he looked like a nice guy. But after about an hour I was despairing. He went on and on about himself and his family, his son, his brother, his life, his work and he barely asked me a single question. When he did he didn't even bother listening to the answer but would say things like 'Oh yes, well of course when that happened to me I did bla bla bla'. It was almost funny because it was so obvious. I'd read about men behaving like that but I don't think I'd ever seen it so blatantly. We didn't have another date."

Kate

TOPICS TO AVOID

I don't think it's a good idea to say "Don't talk about this, this or this" on your first date, because nothing will make you more nervous than trying to remember a list of things you're 'not allowed' to talk about.

There are no hard and fast rules, but I would say go easy on the information you give away about yourself and your family until you know your date well. And also be careful what you say about past relationships.

By the age of 40 all of us have picked up a bit of 'life experience' along the way. Some have had some pretty horrendous experiences, others have had bad luck. Whatever your circumstances there are bound to be a few stories, but the first date is not always the best time to recount them.

If your date is interested in why you're single and dating then it's fair enough to say your marriage didn't work out and you got divorced a few years ago. Or say you were with someone when you were younger but it didn't work out and you haven't met a significant partner since. If you're widowed and you're happy for them to know this then say so, but spare them the details of an agonising bereavement until they know you a little better, otherwise it could get awkward.

There's nothing *wrong* with being totally honest and spilling the beans about how your husband had an affair with your next-door neighbour or how your wife ran off with her boss – but your date may feel it's far more information than he/she wanted to hear straight away.

Also, for security's sake, don't give away too much about your personal details and family until you know the person a lot better. In particular don't let them have your home address until you're really confident that you trust them – and probably not until you've met some of their friends or family. (See more in the safety chapter.)

If you are a parent your date will know you have children unless you've been spectacularly dishonest about it. And if you didn't own up to being a parent before your first date then you probably won't have any further dates once you admit it. There's absolutely no point in lying about having children. People who don't want to date a parent are not going to hang around when they discover you weren't being honest.

If you have been up front about it and your date is relaxed with the idea, it's still probably not the best idea to sit and chatter on and on about what they're doing at school, how funny they are and what their boyfriends or girlfriends are like. Your date is really not going to be that interested – he or she wants to get to know *you*. If they like you then as time passes they'll get to know your children too and hopefully they will all like each other. But don't force the issue – remember this is your date and it's something you are doing independently of your children.

It may be quite an unusual situation for you if you've been bringing children up on your own for a while, but indulge yourself – concentrate on you and your date and try and forget about them for a while. If this date turns into a relationship then they're going to get involved soon enough, so don't rush it.

IF IT ALL GOES WELL

You've arrived, you're looking great and the conversation flows. At this point you're probably looking at your date wondering when the thunderbolt will strike (unless of course you've struck gold and your eyes are locked across a crowded room with your heart a flutter in the best Mills & Boon fashion). Let's assume this isn't the case because it's really pretty unlikely.

If you are having an enjoyable time, the conversation is easy and there isn't anything about this person that instantly turns you off, then go for a second date. All the experts say people behave very differently on a second date and it's only then that you get a true feeling for who that person is.

Why are people different on a second date? Because you're both more relaxed, you have more to talk about, you are more confident about your choice of clothes/hair/make-up. Quite simply, you know what to expect and are less nervous.

But how do you propose a second date? Should you admit to it on date one or should you wait till later and phone or email? Again, no hard and fast rules here. But if you have got the feeling that the date has gone well then it's perfectly fine to say "I've had a really nice time, let's do it again soon." Or "I enjoyed that, shall we meet up again?"

Don't put pressure on for a time and place – your date may want to go home and think about it – but don't try too hard to play it cool. Remember, when you're nervous it's really easy to misinterpret signals and your date could think you're not interested and never get in touch with you again if you're too stand-offish.

Some 'dating experts' say that men still expect to be the one to call the shots and they should be the ones who propose a second date. Women should bow to their alpha male streak and let them think they're in control.

I'm not convinced. I think you should follow your instincts. If you had a great time and he seemed to enjoy himself too, then say so. Guys, if you enjoyed your date and have every intention of proposing a second date, tell her before you leave that you hope you'll see her again. It doesn't have to be a firm arrangement, but an indication that you're going to call will send her away feeling happy and confident.

SOME TIPS FOR THE ALL-IMPORTANT SECOND DATE

Moving on to date two, arrange to take a little more time so you can get to know each other more thoroughly. You could have lunch or dinner, go to an exhibition or go for a walk.

Be careful with dinner – meeting in the evening can lead to an awkward moment when it's time to go home, if you're not careful. A man is likely to offer to see a woman home to make sure she's safe, but you may not want him to know where you live, or be put in an awkward situation at the end of an evening. Lunch is probably easier. It's quite likely you'll be going on somewhere else afterwards and there isn't the danger factor of going home alone late at night.

I think a walk is a great idea, especially if one of you has a dog. Somehow it's easier to talk when you're walking than when you're stuck at a table across from one another. Also, if there is a pause in the conversation it's never quite as obvious when you're walking, and you can always find something to talk about in the view or your surroundings. If the weather's not great you have the perfect excuse to go for a nice hot drink or glass of wine when you've walked as well.

Exhibitions are the same: lots of material for conversation, easy pauses as you look at the exhibits and plenty to discuss afterwards over coffee or lunch.

It's probably best to leave potential tennis games or running sessions until later – it's a bit early to see each other in sweaty sports gear.

The aim with date number two is to get more of an idea about this person. Can you sustain a conversation or is there nothing left to talk about once all the basics have been covered? Do you know any people in common? Do you share any interests? Do you see potential for fun weekends and holidays together or are you like chalk and cheese? Does she make you laugh? Do you think you fancy him?

You may well not be struck by a thunderbolt, but sexual chemistry can develop slowly. It's a combination of looks, voice and humour and is an innate, physical reaction that we can't control. Looks play a big part in it but you can just as easily feel chemistry for someone who doesn't fit in with your usual 'type' – and you can never feel it for someone you haven't met.

It's quite possible to begin by fancying someone and end up feeling an overwhelming desire for them that makes your stomach lurch and your heart flutter. But if this doesn't happen the moment you clap eyes on each other don't give up. It's worth taking a little time because it may start to happen as you make more eye contact, laugh at each other's jokes and become more familiar with each other.

So unless you're completely turned off, give it another go. You may be surprised and if date two goes well, you could be on to something. You'll probably have a pretty good feeling after two dates whether you want to spend more time in this person's company or not.

Taking it further

Obviously one of the things on your mind when dating is when do you sleep with a new partner?

The sexual mores of the 21st century are nothing if not confusing and for many people new to the dating game, sex can be a terrifying prospect.

Many people dating in their 50s and 60s may have been married for 20 years or more, may have only had sex with their husband or wife, or perhaps had one or two other partners before getting married – but we might be talking back in the 1970s or even '60s.

Added to the fact that you haven't had very varied experience, you also don't look quite the same as you did when you met your previous partner in the prime of youth.

The first thing to say about this is *don't worry*! Easier said than done maybe, but unless you're dating someone who is 20 years younger than you are then your partner will most probably be feeling *exactly the same* about their own body. And if you are dating someone 20 years younger than you, then they're probably too bowled over by the attention and your experience to worry about your muscle tone.

Yes, your skin might be a bit looser, the muscles a bit less firm, the wrinkles more pronounced. But let's look at the plus points:

You have a wealth of experience that you didn't have at 20. You have lived, worked, travelled, possibly raised a family. You've had great times and been through awful times, you'll have suffered bereavements, seen relationships break down, had difficult periods with children and partners. All of these have given you solid life experience which makes you a more rounded, interesting human being and fascinating to get to know.

You also have more sexual experience than you had when you first dated even if you have only had one or two partners and, hopefully, you know what you like in bed. That should give you confidence – and girls, remember there's nothing more sexy than a woman who is at ease with her own body.

Self-confident women who have a full and interesting life tend to be more relaxed, more natural and laugh more than those whose confidence is lacking, and that alone can be incredibly sexy. It's not all about having long bronzed legs and a killer bust – there's nothing as sexy as a woman who takes pride and care in her appearance, who behaves naturally and is at ease with herself.

And you only have to take one look at a page of personal ads to realise that men and women like their partners to come in all shapes and sizes.

No one can tell you when it's right to sleep with a new partner. You may feel comfortable having sex after a couple of dates – you may want to wait for weeks or even months. One thing's for sure though, when you're dating later in life there's no question that you've both had previous partners and it's not an issue, it's part and parcel of dating when you're older and can make it quite exciting.

You can't pretend you're virginal, but you can be straightforward about not wanting to rush into the bedroom. And as confidence comes with age, there really is no reason to worry about being dumped because you won't have sex. At 40 plus, it's much easier for a woman to have the confidence to say she's not ready to hit the sack than when she's young, desperately in love and eager to please.

However it's not all one-sided. The sex issue is as tricky for men as it is for women. You fancy her, you haven't had sex for a long time, you'd really like to sleep with her. But she's a grandmother, and a respectable one at that. How on earth do you ask her into bed?

You may also be dealing with women who are ... how shall we say this ... not at their most hormonally balanced. It can be a real challenge to understand the menopause, especially if you're with a woman who you don't know that well. After being with someone for 30 years it's probably a little easier to be rational, especially as you know what she was like before the hormone rages started. But with a new partner it can be quite hard to know how to handle it.

Some men will look for younger women to avoid having to cope with the effects of the menopause while others will bravely endure the flushes and mood swings in the hope of calmer waters to follow.

Needless to say, there are plenty of issues that can complicate sex for older daters, even if the worries of inexperience and unwanted pregnancy have long been laid to rest.

Male impotence is a classic. It's very common and happens more in older men than those in their prime. It can be a classic sign of problems such as high blood pressure, diabetes or cardiovascular disease and can also be caused by factors such as smoking or drinking, stress, nerves, guilt, bereavement or tiredness. If you experience it then go and see your GP. It may be embarrassing to talk about, but it's worth having your health checked out and there could be an easy remedy.

Equally important is to talk openly with your partner. If you don't talk about it, and avoid having sex because of it, your partner is likely to think you are not interested in her which will harm your relationship more than the impotence.

You can still embark on an extremely pleasurable sex life by not focusing on intercourse but finding other ways to please your partner. Make her feel desired and special and she probably won't find the impotence an issue. And if you're able to relax and be open with each other about it, you're more likely to get over the problem too.

One word of warning though: there is one side-effect of sex that you may not have thought much about 30 years ago but which is more worrying than ever – sexually transmitted diseases.

Even if you are way past the age of conceiving a child, you should still practise safe sex and use a condom. Cases of gonorrhoea and syphilis are rising in the over 65 age bracket, so be sensible.

Don't feel pressured into doing anything you don't want, but be brave enough to know that it's OK to have sex. More than that, it's fun – and it's good for you. Sex is a proven stress-reliever and people with good sex lives live longer and have better health.

You're older, you don't have to be home by 10 o'clock, you're with someone you like – so if you both fancy each other then sex will hopefully be a fulfilling part of a great relationship.

The only problem now is how to keep up an active sex life when the grandchildren come to visit.

CHAPTER 9

THE BIOLOGICAL CLOCK

One of the issues we face as older adults back in the dating game is that of age.

There are many examples in this book of people who have found new partners who were unexpectedly older or younger than themselves. People who fell outside their 'ideal' age bracket.

We all know that once you get into your thirties the age gap does narrow and what seemed like a gulf between 15 and 23, say, is virtually unnoticeable between 35 and 43.

The fact that people end up in relationships with partners who are much older than their ideal shows that you really can't predict who you'll fall in love with – and you should be careful not to rule anyone out.

But how does age affect dating and relationships when you get past the first flush of adulthood?

Every professional in the dating game that I spoke to agreed that men all want to meet a younger woman. And, while men of 50 still want to meet women in their thirties, few women want to meet a man who is more than five years older than them, which presents a bit of a conundrum.

Men who have focused on a career and haven't had children by the age of 40 or 45 still think there's time if they meet a woman who is in her thirties.

Yet men who don't want to have a child – or have more children – can be nervous of women in their thirties who they may suspect are on the lookout for a potential father.

For women in their late thirties and early forties it's no simpler. If you want to have children it's hard to ignore that thought when you meet potential partners, even on the first date.

> *"It's very difficult to have a normal first date and get to know someone slowly when you're thinking from the minute you set eyes on him 'could I let this man be the father of my children'?"* Joanne

But if you really don't want to have children, or are not seriously concerned if you don't, or perhaps you know you can't have children, then how do you convince potential dates of this without getting into ridiculously heavy conversations via the internet or on date one?

It's best, as a starting point, to make sure you answer the question about children on any internet profile you complete with total honesty. If you'd like kids, then say so – there's usually a tick box that asks this question.

And you need to be realistic about what other people are looking for and accept that too.

> *"OK, so you are a 48 year old woman – beautiful, confident and a joy to be with. And you may well attract younger men when you go out for a night. But if their profile says the 43 year old you have your eye on definitely wants children, then accept that you don't meet his requirements. Don't put yourself up for unnecessary disappointment. There's no point and it's a waste of energy."* Denise

Likewise, if you really don't want to date someone who either has, or wants, children then it's probably best to make this clear in your profile too.

There's not a lot of point getting involved in a relationship with someone who has diametrically opposed opinions on this subject as it'll only come unstuck at some point in the future. Unfortunately, this is one issue on which you just can't meet in the middle.

> *"Some of my friends are so desperate to have a baby you can almost smell it on them. I do love kids but I don't feel so strongly about it that it's more important to me than meeting someone I know I could share my life with. Men completely write you off if you're over 33 and under 45. They figure the only thing you want to do is have a baby. I think it scares the hell out of them. Then there are guys who want to have a baby and look at your 38-year-old ovaries and think 'Nah, I'm gonna go younger'."*
> Stephanie

The experts' view

Claire Gillbanks says it's the men who are losing out when they insist on finding younger women to date. "Men over 40 are missing a trick with women over 30. They're missing out on a whole population of people who are still experienced and attractive.

"Also, women over 40 have a different approach to dating because they don't have the worry about fertility, they're not looking for a father figure and they haven't got the pressure of looking for someone to have children with. Those women can stay true to what they're looking for."

Fiona Maclean said in her experience of running dating websites she's seen a lot of men in their 40s having relationships 'of sorts' with women the same age. "But they never commit to it because they want to meet someone to have kids with."

Yet for those men who are not desperate to start a family, they could really be missing a trick by insisting on going for younger women.

"One thing that's so enjoyable about dating in later life is that the whole thing is relatively easy, compared to finding a partner when you're young. It's so much simpler when you get to our age because when you're in your 20s a partner has to tick so many boxes. They have to love you, you have to love them, you have to be able to build a home together, you may want to have kids together, build a life together, it might be important that your family gets on with them. But in your 40s or 50s all that is dealt with, and all you're looking for is someone who makes you happy. That's the only box you have to tick."
Colette

And you don't have to get your dad's permission to see them on a Saturday night. You couldn't ask for much more than that.

CHAPTER 10

DATE SAFETY

It's a sad fact that dating can, occasionally, be a dangerous game. Meeting strangers after dark on your own, when nobody knows where you are, is obviously not the brightest idea and not something you would normally do. But if you follow some basic common sense you are unlikely to run into any problems at all.

Remember, dating is supposed to be fun, so keep it safe and it will be.

I've listed some fundamentals that anyone going to meet a new date for the first time should keep in mind. These go for both men and women. They may sound over-cautious, but it's much better to be safe than sorry until you've got to know your date a little.

◆ Arrange your first date to be during the day, in daylight, in public.

◆ Never invite someone to your own house or arrange to meet in a secluded or private place.

◆ Don't drink too much – you could impair your judgment.

◆ Take your mobile phone with you and keep it switched on. Make sure the batteries are charged.

◆ Make sure you have money with you.

◆ Make sure someone knows where you are going to meet your date and if possible give a friend your date's mobile phone number before you go.

◆ Tell a friend where you met the date – which internet dating site or through which singles organisation if it was at a party or event.

◆ Make sure you know how you're going to get home.

◆ Pick a venue close to a bus stop or train station, or drive in your own car so you don't drink.

◆ Don't let your date pick you up at your house or drive you home after a first date.

◆ Keep an eye on your drink. The incidence of drinks being spiked so that someone becomes sleepy and unaware of what is happening to them is higher amongst young people, but it's worth being aware of it nevertheless.

There are also some general safety tips that you might want to consider if you're involved in internet dating in particular:

◆ Think about keeping a spare mobile phone that you can use just for conversations with potential dates. If someone becomes a pain and starts hassling you then you can cut the number off without having to change your main mobile number.

◆ Keep a separate email address for dating. Again, if someone starts sending unwanted messages you can just delete the account and set up a new one. You can set up as many free accounts as you like at **www.gmail.com** or **www.hotmail.com**.

This piece of advice is, unfortunately, more relevant to women than men: if you are going to invite a date to your house or go to theirs, tell a friend beforehand and arrange a time to speak to them afterwards. While you may not want your friends to know exactly what is going on in your love life, it is a good idea for someone to know where you are, just in case something goes wrong.

This is all rather depressing but, as I said above, as long as you follow some basic rules you should be able to go out and enjoy your dating without worrying about any of this. Just follow your common sense and your gut instincts and you should have a great time.

All that remains is for me to wish you luck on your dating journey – and remember, this is supposed to be fun.

Go out there, and let them know how fabulous you are!

Caroline

X

Useful contacts

We've put together a list of useful websites if you're joining the dating game. As contact details often change we've put the list on our website where we can update it regularly, rather than printed it here. You can find the list at **www.white ladderpress.com**; click on 'useful contacts' next to the information about this book.

If you don't have access to the internet you can contact White Ladder Press by any of the means listed on the next page and we'll print off a hard copy and post it to you free of charge.

Contact us

You're welcome to contact White Ladder Press if you have any questions or comments for either us or the authors. Please use whichever of the following routes suits you.

Phone: 01803 813343

Email: enquiries@whiteladderpress.com

Fax: 0208 334 1601

Address: 2nd Floor, Westminster House, Kew Road, Richmond, Surrey TW9 2ND

Website: www.whiteladderpress.com

What can our website do for you?

If you want more information about any of our books, you'll find it at **www.whiteladderpress.com**. In particular you'll find extracts from each of our books, and reviews of those that are already published. We also run special offers on future titles if you order online before publication. And you can request a copy of our free catalogue.

Many of our books have links pages, useful addresses and so on relevant to the subject of the book. You'll also find out a bit more about us and, if you're a writer yourself, you'll find our submission guidelines for authors. So please check us out and let us know if you have any comments, questions or suggestions.

Diary of a Reluctant Green

Can you save the planet and have a life?

"I loved this book! A truly practical guide for any self-confessed 'eco-virgin' – informative and witty, realistic yet inspirational." JANEY LEE GRACE, author of *Imperfectly Natural Woman*

Most of us know we need to be greener than we are now. We know that the world is suffering and it's down to us as individuals to take action. But, well, it's just a giant hassle isn't it? Three bins in the kitchen for recycling, energy saving light bulbs (which just aren't the same), remembering your canvas bag to go shopping … I mean, come on, it's not as if one person can make that much of a difference, is it?

You're not alone. There's something about that sanctimonious eco-zealot brigade that puts you off the whole idea. But actually, the guilt does get to you sometimes and of course you'd like to do your bit if you could find the energy (from a renewable source, obviously).

Richard Hallows was very unconvinced that he could sustain the motivation to go green, or that his small contribution to the planet's welfare would be worth having. However, guilt and a desire to reduce his household bills persuaded him, reluctantly, to give it a try. This is his diary of the first few months of going green – funny, cynical and full of practical tips for:
- saving money by being greener
- finding shortcuts that remove the hassle
- working out where it's worth putting your efforts – and where it isn't

He's not always convinced by the arguments, he's driven mad by the contradictions in eco-guidelines, and he doesn't always succeed. But he reveals how his family manages to save the planet at least a little bit, without having to knit their own pasta or wear sandals.

£7.99

The OUTDOOR POCKET BIBLE

EVERY OUTDOOR RULE OF THUMB *at your fingertips*

PAUL JENNER & CHRISTINE SMITH

When you're out and about enjoying the countryside the last thing you need is to lug around several different guides to wildlife, geology, meteorology, and any other 'ology. But there are plenty of things you'd like to look up if you could. How do you light a fire when all the wood is wet? Are those fox tracks or dog tracks? Is it going to rain?

Generally there's nothing you can do but hope for the best, or maybe phone a friend if you can get reception, and they're in, and they know the answer...

That's where this book is so brilliant. It has the answers to more questions than you'd think could fit into such a handy volume. You'll find out pretty much anything you need to know:

◆ Emergency advice, from basic first aid to how to escape from quicksand
◆ Help with navigation, such as telling which way is north by your watch, or by the moon
◆ Identification guides: constellations, seashells and shore life, semi-precious stones, burial mounds, animal tracks and more
◆ Boating guidelines, from tides to tying knots to what the buoys mean
◆ Which wild food you can eat and how to recognise it
◆ Weather lore, such as which clouds indicate what kind of weather

This is the only book you really can't do without when you're out and about. So you can ditch that library of guidebooks and slip this in your pocket instead.

Price £7.99